GEO

My iPhone®

Brad Miser

que®

800 East 96th Street,
Indianapolis, Indiana 46240 USA

My iPhone

Copyright © 2008 by Que Publishing

ISBN-13: 978-0-7897-3726-7
ISBN-10: 0-7897-3726-4

Library of Congress Cataloging-in-Publication Data

Miser, Brad.

  My iPhone / Brad Miser.

    p. cm.

  ISBN 0-7897-3726-4

  1. iPhone (Smartphone) 2. Cellular telephones. 3. Digital music players. 4. Pocket computers. I. Title.

  TK6570.M6M535 2008

  621.3845'6—dc22

                    2007036724

Printed in the United States on America

First Printing: October 2007

Trademarks

All terms mentioned in this book that are known to be trademarks or service marks have been appropriately capitalized. Que Publishing cannot attest to the accuracy of this information. Use of a term in this book should not be regarded as affecting the validity of any trademark or service mark.

iPhone is a trademark of Apple, Inc.

Warning and Disclaimer

Every effort has been made to make this book as complete and as accurate as possible, but no warranty or fitness is implied. The information provided is on an "as is" basis. The author and the publisher shall have neither liability nor responsibility to any person or entity with respect to any loss or damages arising from the information contained in this book.

Bulk Sales

Que Publishing offers excellent discounts on this book when ordered in quantity for bulk purchases or special sales. For more information, please contact

   U.S. Corporate and Government Sales
   1-800-382-3419
   corpsales@pearsontechgroup.com

For sales outside of the U.S., please contact

   International Sales
   international@pearsoned.com

ASSOCIATE PUBLISHER
Greg Wiegand

ACQUISITIONS AND DEVELOPMENT EDITOR
Laura Norman

MANAGING EDITOR
Gina Kanouse

PROJECT EDITOR
Jovana San Nicolas-Shirley

COPY EDITOR
Mike Henry

INDEXER
Cheryl Lenser

PROOFREADER
Language Logistics, LLC
San Dee Phillips

TECHNICAL EDITOR
Griff Partington

BOOK DESIGNER
Anne Jones

COMPOSITION
Gloria Schurick

GRAPHICS
Tammy Graham

This Book Is Safari Enabled

The Safari® Enabled icon on the cover of your favorite technology book means the book is available through Safari Bookshelf.

When you buy this book, you get free access to the online edition for 45 days.

Safari Bookshelf is an electronic reference library that lets you easily search thousands of technical books, find code samples, download chapters, and access technical information whenever and wherever you need it.

To gain 45-day Safari Enabled access to this book:

- Go to http://www.quepublishing.com/safarienabled
- Complete the brief registration form
- Enter the coupon code 6NGH-Y9WF-5X91-4PFJ-HRDE

If you have difficulty registering on Safari Bookshelf or accessing the online edition, please e-mail customer service@safaribooksonline.com.

Contents at a Glance

Table of Contents

About the Author

Brad Miser has written extensively about technology, with his favorite topics being the amazing "i" gadgets, iPhone and iPod, which make it possible to take our lives with us while we are on the move. In addition to *My iPhone*, Brad has written many other books, including *Absolute Beginner's Guide to iPod and iTunes*; *Sleeping with the Enemy: Running Windows on a Mac* (digital Shortcut); *Special Edition Using Mac OS X, v10.4 Tiger*; *Absolute Beginner's Guide to Homeschooling*; *Mac OS X and iLife: Using iTunes, iPhoto, iMovie, and iDVD*; *iDVD 3 Fast & Easy*; *Special Edition Using Mac OS X v10.2*; and *Using Mac OS 8.5*. He has also been an author, development editor, or technical editor on more than 50 other titles. He has written numerous articles in *MacAddict* magazine and has been a featured speaker on various topics at Macworld Expo, at user group meetings, and in other venues.

Brad is or has been a sales support specialist, the director of product and customer services, and the manager of education and support services for several software development companies. Previously, he was the lead proposal specialist for an aircraft engine manufacturer, a development editor for a computer book publisher, and a civilian aviation test officer/engineer for the U.S. Army. Brad holds a Bachelor of Science degree in mechanical engineering from California Polytechnic State University in San Luis Obispo and has received advanced education in maintainability engineering, business, and other topics.

In addition to his passion for silicon-based technology, Brad likes to ride his steel-based technology, AKA motorcycle, whenever and wherever possible.

A native of California, Brad now lives in Brownsburg, Indiana, with his wife Amy; their three daughters, Jill, Emily, and Grace; and a rabbit named Bun-Bun.

Brad would love to hear about your experiences with this book (the good, the bad, and the ugly). You can write to him at bradmacosx@mac.com.

Dedication

To those who have given the last full measure of devotion so that the rest of us can be free.

Acknowledgments

To the following people on the *My iPhone* project team, my sincere appreciation for your hard work on this book:

Laura Norman, my acquisitions and development editor, who enhanced the concept for this book and brought it to fruition.

Marta Justak of Justak Literary Services, my agent, for getting me signed up for this project.

Griff Partington, my technical editor, who did a great job to ensure that the information in this book is both accurate and useful.

Jill, Emily, and Grace Miser who helped with figure preparation.

Mike Henry, my copy editor, who corrected my many misspellings, poor grammar, and other problems.

Jovana San Nicolas-Shirley, my project editor, who skillfully managed the hundreds of files that it took to make this book.

Anne Jones, for the interior design and cover of this book.

Que's production and sales team for printing this book and getting it into your hands.

We Want to Hear from You!

As the reader of this book, *you* are our most important critic and commentator. We value your opinion and want to know what we're doing right, what we could do better, what areas you'd like to see us publish in, and any other words of wisdom you're willing to pass our way.

As an associate publisher for Que Publishing, I welcome your comments. You can email or write me directly to let me know what you did or didn't like about this book—as well as what we can do to make our books better.

Please note that I cannot help you with technical problems related to the topic of this book. We do have a User Services group, however, where I will forward specific technical questions related to the book.

When you write, please be sure to include this book's title and author as well as your name, email address, and phone number. I will carefully review your comments and share them with the author and editors who worked on the book.

Email: feedback@quepublishing.com

Mail: Greg Wiegand
Associate Publisher
Que Publishing
800 East 96th Street
Indianapolis, IN 46240 USA

Reader Services

Visit our website and register this book at www.quepublishing.com/register for convenient access to any updates, downloads, or errata that might be available for this book.

Prologue

P

Getting Started with iPhone

The good news is that getting started with an iPhone is a simple, painless process. You've got your hands on one, so it's time to get going.

Preparing iTunes

Before you can use the iPhone, you have to download and install iTunes on your computer or make sure that if you are using the most current version if it's already installed. To get started, jump into any of the following sections that apply to your particular situation.

Downloading and Installing iTunes on a Windows PC

1. Open a web browser.

2. Move to www.apple.com/itunes.

3. Click the Download iTunes button. You move to the Download iTunes screen.

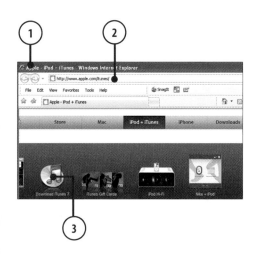

4. Uncheck the two check boxes.

5. Click Download iTunes Free. The installer application starts.

6. Follow the onscreen instructions to install iTunes.

Mac Installation Section Missing?

If you happen to be wondering why there isn't a section on installing iTunes on a Mac, it's because Macs come with iTunes pre-installed. If you weren't wondering, never mind.

Updating iTunes

1. Open iTunes.

2. On a Windows PC, choose Help, Check for Updates. On a Mac, choose iTunes, Check for Updates. The application checks your version of iTunes against the current version.

3. If you are using the current version, click OK to clear the dialog telling you so. If you aren't using the current version, you're prompted to download and install it. Follow the onscreen instructions to download and install the newer version.

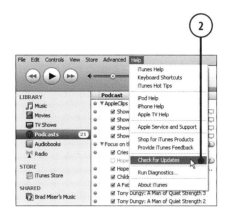

Obtaining and Signing in to an iTunes Store Account

1. Open iTunes.

2. Click iTunes Store. You connect to the Internet and move into the iTunes Store.

3. Click Sign In. The Sign In dialog appears.

Already Logged In?

If you see an Apple ID instead of the Sign In button, iTunes is already logged into an iTunes Store account. If the account is yours, skip the rest of these steps. If the account isn't yours, click the account shown and click Sign Out so that you can create or sign in to your own account.

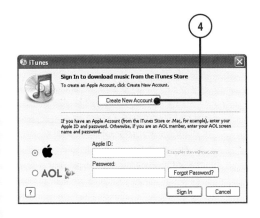

4. Click Create New Account. You move to the first screen in the account creation process.

5. Read the information and follow the onscreen instructions to create an Apple ID. After you complete the steps, you receive your Apple ID and password.

Got iTunes Store Account?
You can log in to an existing iTunes Store account by entering your Apple ID and password and then clicking Sign In. Skip the rest of these steps.

Installing and Activating iPhone

Get ready for this part of the process by taking all the goodies out of iPhone's box. For now, you'll need the phone, the USB-to-Dock cable, and the Dock. Take all the protective plastic off each item.

>>>step-by-step

1. Connect the USB end of the cable to an available USB port on your computer.

2. Connect the other end of the cable to the Dock.

3. Gently place the iPhone into the Dock by sliding its bottom into the Dock until it connects. When it connects, you see the Apple logo on the iPhone as it starts up. The Activation screen appears briefly, iTunes becomes active on your computer, and your iPhone appears on the iTunes Source list and in the Content pane.

4. Click Continue. You see the AT&T account screen prompting you to choose whether you are a new or existing AT&T customer. If you are a new customer, you have to create an account with AT&T and activate one or more iPhones. If you already have an AT&T account, you can replace your current account with iPhone or add it as a new line. For simplicity's sake, the rest of these steps assume that you are a new customer and are activating one iPhone. The other scenarios work out the same way—just read and follow the onscreen instructions.

5. Select the AT&T account option applicable to you.

6. Click Continue. What you see depends on the option you selected; the rest of these steps assume that you are new to AT&T and are activating a single iPhone. You move to the Transfer Your Mobile Number screen that enables you to move an existing number onto iPhone.

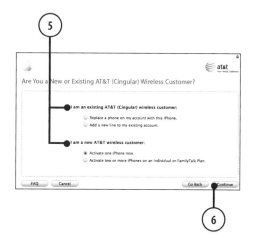

Not So Fast

If other applications, such as iPhoto on a Mac, open when you connect the iPhone, quit them until you've activated the iPhone.

7. If you want to move an existing number onto the iPhone, complete the form. If you want a new number, leave the form empty. Click Continue.

If you choose to move an existing number onto the iPhone, the activation process can take up to six hours. The rest of these steps assume that you are putting a new number on the iPhone.

You see the Select Your Monthly AT&T Plan screen. The plans you see depend on where you live, but the information should be self-explanatory. At press time, the differences between the plans were monthly cost versus talk time; all plans included unlimited data access.

You can also add more text messages to your account if you need them. At press time, all accounts included 200 text messages per month.

8. Select the plan and text message options you want and click Continue. You see the iTunes Account screen.

9. Enter your Apple ID and Password and click Continue.

Sooner or Later, You'll Need an Apple ID

If you didn't already create an Apple ID, leave the form blank and click Continue. You're led through the creation of an iTunes Store account, which you must have to activate an iPhone.

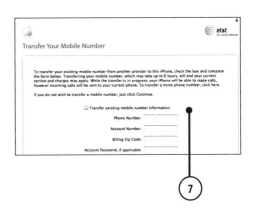

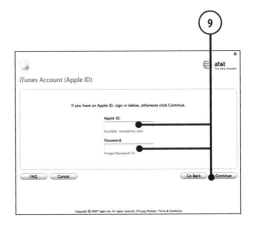

10. Enter or confirm information as you are prompted, and click Continue. You see the Billing Information screen.

11. Provide the required billing information and click Continue.

    If prompted to confirm your address, do so and click Continue. After you provided all necessary information, the terms and conditions screen appears.

12. If you have hours to kill and are legally minded, read the terms and conditions; when you're done, check the check box and click Continue and then repeat the process with the next legal screen. You see the Review Your Information screen.

13. If everything looks correct, click Continue. You see the activation processing screen on your computer and on your iPhone.

    When the process is complete, you see the Completing Activation screen. The most important bit of information on this screen is your new phone number.

    AT&T begins activating your iPhone. When it is active, you see the iPhone is activated screen on your iPhone.

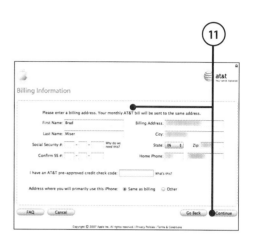

14. Click Continue. You see the Set Up Your iPhone screen.

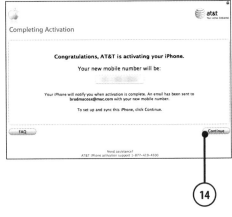

15. Enter a name for your iPhone in the Name field.

16. If you want your calendars, contacts, email accounts, and so on to sync, leave the check box checked.

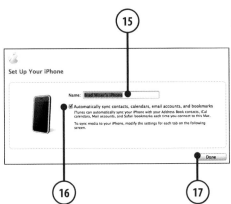

17. Click Done. iTunes moves the information from your computer onto iPhone. You see the sync progress screens on your computer and on iPhone.

After iPhone is active, set up, and in sync, you can start using all its great features. You'll want to start by learning to use its cell phone features, moving iTunes music and video onto it, syncing podcasts, and so on. And that's where the rest of this book comes in.

iPhone Memory Not Unlimited

If you leave the check box checked in step 16, it is likely that not all information will fit onto iPhone unless your iTunes Library is fairly small. If all the content can't be moved onto iPhone, you see prompts explaining this and suggesting what you can do to complete the sync. (*Sync* is the action of moving data between iPhone and computers.) Just follow the onscreen instructions to complete the sync process. Later in this book, you learn how to be selective about what moves to iPhone so that the data on iPhone is what you want.

Touring iPhone

Take a quick look at iPhone's physical controls and ports and learn how you move around its screens.

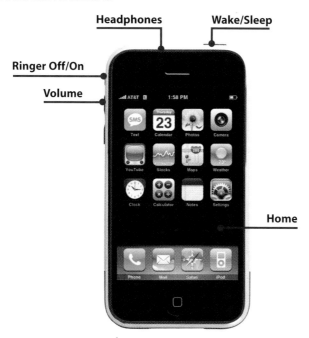

• **Ringer Off/On**   This switch determines whether iPhone rings when a call comes in. Slide it toward the front of iPhone to hear the ringer; a Bell icon appears on the screen to indicate the ringer is on. Slide it toward the back of iPhone to turn the ringer off; a red dot appears on the switch, and the bell with a line through it appears on iPhone's screen to indicate that the ringer is off.

- **Volume**   Press the upper part of the rocker switch to increase volume; press the lower part of the switch to decrease volume. The volume that is controlled depends on what you are doing. If iPhone isn't busy, its ringer volume is controlled. If you are listening to music or watching video, the volume of what you are listening to or watching is controlled. If you are talking on the phone, the volume of the call is controlled.

- **Dock**   Use this port to connect iPhone into its Dock or to connect the cable directly to iPhone.

- **Home**   Press this button to move to the all-important iPhone Home screen.

- **Wake/Sleep**   Press this to lock iPhone's controls and to turn off its screen. Press it again to start using iPhone. Note that if you are using iPhone to listen to music when you press this, the music keeps playing while iPhone is locked. You also use this button to turn iPhone off and turn it off again.

- **Headphones**   Plug iPhone's headphones into this port.

- **Camera**   iPhone's camera lens is located on its backside near the top.

When iPhone is locked and you press the Wake/Sleep button or the Home button, iPhone's screen activates, and you see the Unlock slider. Drag your finger to the right to unlock iPhone so that you can work with it. You move to the iPhone Home screen or to the last screen you were using.

Locked

Drag to the right to unlock iPhone.

In most cases, you should just put iPhone to sleep when you aren't using it instead of shutting it off. It doesn't use much power when it sleeps but will wake up quickly when you want to start using it again.

Setting ringer volume

To change iPhone's volume, press the up or down volume buttons. An icon pops up to show you which volume you are changing and the relative volume setting. When the volume is set, release the volume button.

Drag to the right to shut down iPhone.

If you want to turn iPhone off, press and hold the Wake/Sleep button until the red slider appears on the screen. Drag the slider to the right to shut iPhone down.

To restart iPhone, press and hold the Wake/Sleep button until the Apple logo appears on the screen. In a moment, you see iPhone's Home screen, and it's ready for you to use again.

The Time Is Always Handy

If you use iPhone as a watch, the way I do, just press the Wake/Sleep button. The current time and date appear; if you don't unlock it, iPhone goes back to sleep.

Using This Book

This book has been designed to help you transform iPhone into *your* iPhone by helping you learn to use it easily and quickly. As you can tell, the book relies heavily on pictures to show you how iPhone works. It is also task-focused so that you can quickly learn the specific steps to follow to do all the cool things you can do with iPhone.

Using iPhone involves touching its screen with your fingers. When you need to press part of the screen, such as a button or keyboard, you see a callout with the step number pointing to where you need to press. When you need to drag or slide your finger along the screen, such as to browse lists, you see the following icon:

The directions you can drag are indicated with arrows.

To zoom in or zoom out on screens, you unpinch or pinch, respectively, your fingers on the screen. These motions are indicated by the following icons:

Because iTunes and iPhone work with both Windows computers and Macs, this book is designed for both platforms as well. When there are significant differences, such as applications you use to store photos, you see task sections devoted to each type of computer. You can safely skip over sections focused on a type of computer you don't use.

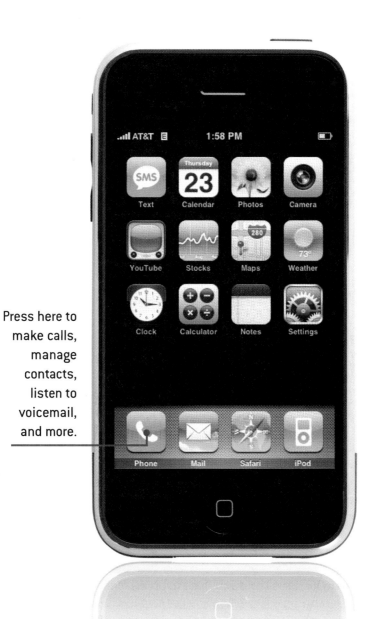

Press here to make calls, manage contacts, listen to voicemail, and more.

In this chapter, you'll explore all the cell phone functionality that iPhone has to offer. The topics include the following:

→ Configuring phone settings
→ Making calls
→ Receiving calls
→ Managing calls
→ Using visual voicemail

Making, Receiving, and Managing Calls

Although it's also a lot of other great things, such as an iPod, web browser, email tool, and such, there's a reason the word *phone* is in iPhone's name. It's a feature-rich cell phone including one of iPhone's best features, which is visual voicemail. Other useful features include a speaker phone, conference calling, and easy-to-use onscreen controls. Plus, iPhone's phone functions are integrated with its other features. For example, when using the Maps widget, you might find a location, such as a business, that you're interested in contacting. You can call that location just by pressing the number you want to call directly from the Maps widget screen. (Chapter 10, "Using Other iPhone Widgets," covers the Maps widget.) No need to fumble around switching to phone mode and dialing the number manually. iPhone makes your mobile phone use quicker, easier, and smarter in other ways, as you'll see in the pages that follow.

Configuring Phone Settings

Before jumping into iPhone calling, take a few minutes to configure iPhone's phone functions to work the way you want them to. To start, move to iPhone's Home screen by pressing the Home button at the bottom of iPhone. On the Home screen, press Settings. The Settings screen appears.

Press to configure sound settings.

Press to configure phone settings.

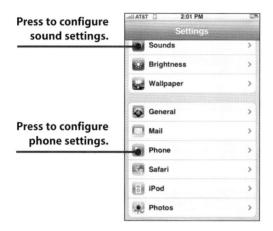

>>>*step-by-step*

Setting Phone Sounds

You can set iPhone to play specific sounds for various events, such as a ringtone, voicemail message, and so on.

1. Press the Home button to move to the home screen.

2. Press Settings.

3. On the Settings screen, press Sounds. The Sounds screen appears.

4. To prevent iPhone from vibrating when you've silenced the ringer, press the Vibrate ON button. The status becomes OFF, and iPhone won't vibrate when you have silenced it using the Ring/Silent switch.

5. To prevent iPhone from vibrating when the ringer is active, press the Vibrate ON button. The status becomes OFF and iPhone won't vibrate when the ringer sounds to indicate you're receiving a call.

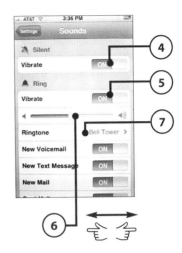

6. To increase the volume level of ringer sounds, drag the slider to the right; drag it to the left to lower the volume of ringer sounds.

7. Press the Ringtone button or the name of the ringtone shown next to that text. The Ringtone screen appears.

8. Listen to a ringtone by pressing its name. The sound is marked with a check mark to show you that it is the current ringtone, and it plays.

9. Drag up and down the screen and keep trying sounds until you find the one you want to use as the ringtone.

10. Press Sounds. You move back to the Sounds screen, and the Ringtone area shows the sound you selected.

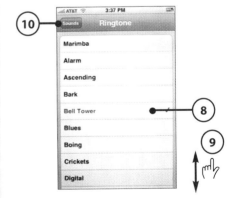

11. If you don't want to hear a sound when you receive a new voice-mail, press ON. It becomes OFF, and you won't hear a sound when you receive voicemail.

12. Press Settings. You move back to the Settings screen.

Hearing Things

If you want to hear any of the sounds, turn that sound off and then press OFF to turn it back on. When you do, you hear the sound that plays when the related event occurs.

It's Not All Good

In its first version, one of the most disappointing features for iPhone's cell phone module is that you can't add new ringtones using iTunes. With your entire iTunes Library available to iPhone, it seems logical that you'd be able to configure any music or sounds in iTunes as ringtones. Unfortunately, in the first edition of iPhone, this isn't possible. (Hopefully, this will change at some point; early versions of iPhone demos showed ringtones being set from iTunes.) If you want to use ringtones other than the default iPhone ring-tones, you must have a separate application, or you have to do some "hacking." For example, on the Mac, iFuntastic enables you to use any audio file, including your iTunes music, as ringtones. However, because Apple does not support these techniques and they are often not thoroughly tested, you do run some risk if you try them. To find applications and detailed instructions for modifying iPhone's ringtones, do a web search for "adding ringtones to iPhone," and you'll find applications and hacking instructions.

Also disappointing is that you can't change the sounds associated with new voicemails, text messages, and so on. You can only turn these sounds off and on.

Configuring Phone Settings ▶

1. Press the Home button to move to the Home screen.

2. Press Settings.

3. Drag down the Settings screen until you see Phone.

4. Press Phone. The Phone screen appears. Your number appears at the top of the screen.

5. If you don't want the correct pre-fixes added to U.S. phone numbers when you dial them from outside the United States, press ON. It becomes OFF to show you that you have to add any prefixes manually when dialing a U.S. number from outside the United States.

6. Scroll down until you see Call Forwarding.

7. Press Call Forwarding. The Call Forwarding screen appears.

8. To forward calls, press OFF. It becomes ON to show you that call forwarding is active. The Forwarding To screen appears.

9. Enter the number to which you want to forward calls. Include the number's area code. You can use the special symbols located in the lower-left corner of the keypad to enter pauses and such.

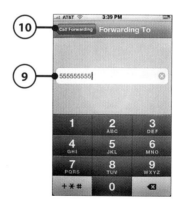

10. Press Call Forwarding. iPhone saves the number, and you return to the Call Forwarding screen. The number to which iPhone will forward calls shows next to the Forwarding To text.

11. Press Phone. You move back to the Phone settings screen.

12. Press Call Waiting. The Call Waiting screen appears.

13. To disable call waiting, press ON. Its status becomes OFF. When call waiting is turned off and you receive a second call while you're already on another call, the second call immediately goes to voicemail.

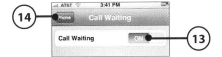

14. Press Phone.

15. Press Show My Caller ID. The Show My Caller ID screen appears.

16. To hide your information when you make calls, press ON. The status becomes OFF to show you that your information won't be transmitted when you make a call. I don't recommend this because it's better to let people know who is calling.

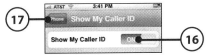

17. Press Phone. You return to the Phone screen and are ready to use iPhone to make and receive calls.

Other Phone Settings

TTY devices enable hearing-impaired people to use a telephone. To use TTY with iPhone, you need an adapter to connect iPhone to a TTY device. You also need to turn TTY support on by pressing the TTY OFF button, which becomes ON to show you that TTY support is active.

The SIM PIN setting enables you to associate a personal ID number, or PIN, with the SIM (subscriber identity module) card in iPhone. You can remove this card from iPhone and install it in other phones that support these cards to be able to use your AT&T account with a different phone. If you set a PIN, that PIN is required to be able to use the card in a different phone.

The AT&T Services option enables you to get information about your account. This is covered at the end of this chapter.

Which Network?

Although iPhone currently supports only the AT&T cell network, when you are in different countries, you might see something other than AT&T next to the strength bars. The specific network you see doesn't really matter; what counts is the strength of the signal you receive. That is, the network you use doesn't matter except for roaming charges, which can be significant depending on where you use iPhone. Before you travel outside of the United States, check with AT&T to determine the roaming rates that apply to where you are going. Also see if there is a discounted roaming plan for that location. If you don't do this before you leave, you might get a nasty surprise when the bill comes in and you see substantial roaming charges.

Making Calls

There are a number of ways to make calls with iPhone, but after a call is in progress, you can manage it in the same way no matter how you started.

>>>step-by-step

Dialing with the Keypad

The most obvious way to make a call is to dial the number.

1. On the Home screen, press Phone. You move to the Phone screen.

2. If you haven't made a call from your current location before, check the signal strength to make sure that you can reach the network. As long as you see at least one bar, you should be able to make and receive calls.

3. Press the Keypad button. The keypad appears if iPhone isn't already displaying it.

4. Press numbers on the keypad to dial the number you want to call.

5. Press Call. iPhone dials the number, and the Call screen appears.

6. Use the Call screen to manage the call; see "Managing In-Process Calls" later in this section for the details.

Dialing with Contacts

iPhone has a complete contact manager so that you can store phone numbers for people and organizations. (You'll learn how to configure your contacts in Chapter 2, "Managing Contacts.") To make a call using a contact, follow these steps.

1. On the Home screen, press Phone. You move to the Phone screen.

Number being dialed

2. If you haven't made a call from your current location before, check the signal strength to make sure that you can reach the network. As long as you see at least one bar, you should be able to make and receive calls.

3. Press the Contacts button. The All Contacts screen appears.

4. Drag your finger up and down to browse the list. The faster you drag up or down, the faster you scroll.

5. To jump to a specific section of the list, click a letter on the index.

6. When you see the contact you want to call, press it. The contact's Info screen appears.

7. Press the number you want to dial. iPhone dials the number, and the Call screen appears.

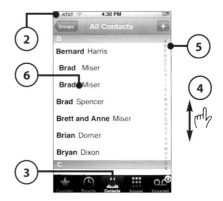

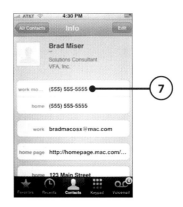

8. Use the Call screen to manage the call; see "Managing In-Process Calls" later in this section for the details.

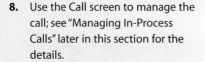

Dialing with Favorites

You can save contacts and phone numbers as favorites to make dialing them even simpler. (You learn how to save favorites in various locations later in this chapter and in Chapter 2.)

1. On the Home screen, press Phone. You move to the Phone screen.

2. If you haven't made a call from your current location before, check the signal strength to make sure that you can reach the network. As long as you see at least one bar, you should be able to make and receive calls.

3. Press the Favorites button. The Favorites screen appears.

4. Drag up or down the list until you see the favorite you want to call.

5. Press the favorite you want to call. iPhone dials the number, and the Call screen appears.

6. Use the Call screen to manage the call; see "Managing In-Process Calls" later in this section for the details.

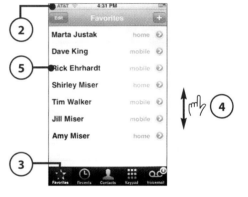

Dialing with Recents

As you make, receive, or miss calls,
iPhone keeps tracks of all the numbers for you. You can use the recent
list to make calls.

1. On the Home screen, press Phone.
   You move to the Phone screen.

2. If you haven't made a call from
   your current location before,
   check the signal strength to make
   sure that you can reach the network. As long as you see at least
   one bar, you should be able to
   make and receive calls.

3. Press the Recents button. The
   Recents screen appears.

4. Press All to see all calls.

5. Press Missed to see only calls you
   missed.

6. Drag your finger up or down the
   screen to browse the list of calls.

7. To call the number associated with
   a recent call, press the title of the
   call, such as a person's name.
   iPhone dials the number, and
   the Call screen appears. Skip to
   step 11.

8. To get more information about a
   recent call, press its Info button.
   The Info screen appears, labeled
   with the type of call, such as
   Outgoing or Missed.

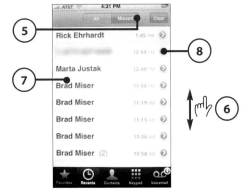

9. Read the information about the call. For example, if the call is related to someone in your contacts list, you see detailed information for that contact. The number associated with the call is highlighted in red.

10. Press a number on the Info screen. iPhone dials the number, and the Call screen appears.

11. Use the Call screen to manage the call; see "Managing In-Process Calls" later in this section for the details.

Going Back

To return to the Recents screen without making a call, press Recent Calls.

Managing In-Process Calls

When you place a call, there are several ways to manage it. The most obvious is to place iPhone next to your ear and use iPhone like any other phone you've ever used. As you place iPhone next to your head, its screen becomes disabled so that you don't accidentally press onscreen buttons. When you take iPhone away from your ear, the Call screen appears again, and iPhone enables its controls.

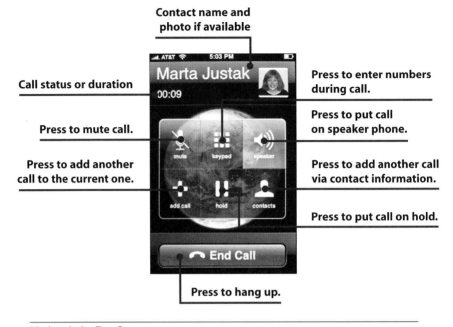

Contact name and photo if available

Call status or duration

Press to enter numbers during call.

Press to mute call.

Press to put call on speaker phone.

Press to add another call to the current one.

Press to add another call via contact information.

Press to put call on hold.

Press to hang up.

Nobody's Perfect

If iPhone can't complete the call for some reason, such as not having a strong enough signal, the Called Failed screen appears. Press Call Back to try again, or press Done to give up. When you press Done, you return to the screen from which you came.

Some of the other things you can do while on a call might not be so obvious, as you'll learn in the next few tasks.

>>>*step-by-step*

Entering Numbers During a Call

You often need to enter numbers during a call, such as to log in to a voice mail system, access an account, and so on.

1. Place a call using any of the methods you've learned so far. The Call screen appears.

2. Press the Keypad button. The keypad appears on the screen.

3. Press the numbers.

4. When you're done, press Hide Keypad. You return to the Call screen.

Making Conference Calls

iPhone makes it easy to talk to multiple people at the same time. You can have two separate calls going on at any point in time. You can have more calls going on by merging them together.

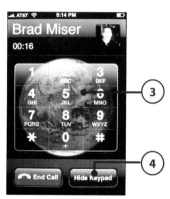

1. Place a call using any of the methods you've learned so far. The Call screen appears.

2. Press add call. The Create a new call screen appears.

Similar but Different

If you press contacts instead of add call, you move directly into the Contacts screen. This might save you one screen press if the person you want to add to the call is in your contacts list.

3. Press the button you want to use to place the next call. Press Favorites to call a favorite, press Recents to use the Recents list, press Contacts to place the call via contacts, or press Keypad to dial the number. These work just as they do when you start a new call.

4. Place the call using the option you selected in step 3. Doing so places the first call on hold and moves you back to the Call screen while iPhone makes the second call. The first call's information appears at the top of the screen, including the word *HOLD* so that you know the call is on hold. iPhone displays the second call just below that, and it is currently the active call.

5. Talk to the second person you called; the first remains on hold.

6. To switch to the first call, press it on the list. This places the second call on hold and moves it to the top of the call list, while the first call becomes active again.

7. To join the calls so that all parties can hear each other, press merge calls. iPhone combines the two calls, and you see a single entry at the top of the screen to reflect this.

First call

Second call

Merging Calls

As you merge calls, iPhone attempts to display the names of the callers at the top of the Call screen. As the text increases, iPhone scrolls it so that you can read it. Eventually, iPhone gives up and replaces the names with the word *Conference*.

8. To add another call, repeat steps 2 though 4. Each time you merge calls, the second line becomes free so that you can add more calls.

9. To manage a conference call, press Conference or the names shown at the top of the screen. The Conference screen appears.

10. To speak with one of the callers privately, press Private. Doing so places the call on hold and returns you to the Call screen showing information about the active call. You can merge the calls again by pressing merge calls.

11. To remove a call from the confer-ence, press the unlock button. The END CALL button appears.

12. To remove a caller from the call, press END CALL. iPhone discon-nects the caller from the confer-ence call. You return to the Call screen and see information about the active call.

13. To move back to the Call screen, press Back. You move to the Call screen and can continue working with the call, such as adding more people to it.

Swap 'em Out

You can also swap calls by press-ing the Swap button.

14. To end the call for all callers, press End Call.

Time Multiplier

When you have multiple calls combined into one, the minutes for each call continue to count individually. So if you've joined three people into one call, each minute of the call counts as three minutes against your calling plan.

Receiving Calls

Receiving calls on iPhone enables you to access the same great tools you can use when you make calls, plus a few more for good measure.

Answering Calls

When iPhone rings, it's time to answer the call—or not. If you configured the ringer to ring, you hear it when a call comes in. If vibrate is turned on, iPhone vibrates whether the ringer is on. And if those two ways aren't enough, a message appears on iPhone's screen to show you information about the incoming call.

Information about who's calling, including photo if available

Send it to voicemail.

Answer the call.

If iPhone is locked when a call comes in, drag the slider to the right to answer it.

Drag to the right to answer.

When you receive a call, you have the following options:

- **Answer** Press Answer to take the call. You move to the Call screen and can work with the call like one you placed from iPhone. For example, you can add a call, merge calls, place the call on hold, end the call, and so on.

- **Decline** If you press Decline, iPhone immediately routes the call to voicemail. You can also decline a call by pressing the Sleep/Wake button twice quickly on iPhone's top.

- **Silence a call** To silence the ringer without sending the call to voicemail, press the Sleep/Wake button on iPhone's top once or press either the upper or lower part of the Volume button on iPhone's left side. The call continues to come in, and you can answer it even though you shut the ringer off for the call.

Silencio!

To turn iPhone's ringer off temporarily, slide the Ringer switch located above the Volume switch on iPhone's left side toward the back so that the red dot appears. The no-ringer icon (a bell with a slash through it) appears on the screen to let you know that you turned the ringer off. To turn it back on again, slide the switch toward iPhone's front. The bell icon appears on the screen to show you that the ringer is active again. To set the ringer's volume, use the Volume switch on iPhone's left side when you aren't in a call and aren't listening to music or video via its iPod functions.

Answering Calls When You're Already on a Call

As you saw earlier, iPhone can manage multiple calls at the same time. If you are on a call and another call comes in, you have a number of ways to respond.

Information about the new call coming in

Press to send incoming call to voicemail.

Press to put current call on hold and answer.

Press to end current call and answer.

- **Decline**   Press Ignore to send the incoming call directly to voicemail.

- **Place the first call on hold and answer the second**   Press Hold Call + Answer to place the current call on hold and answer the second one. After you do this, you can manage the two calls just as when you called two numbers from iPhone. For example, you can place the second call on hold and move back to the first one, merge the calls, add more calls, and so on.

- **End the first call and answer the second**   Press End Call + Answer to terminate the active call and answer the incoming call.

Auto-Mute

If you are listening to music or video, the iPod function automatically pauses when a call comes in. When the call ends, the music or video picks up right where it left off.

Managing Calls

You've already learned most of what you need to know to use iPhone's cell phone functions. In the following sections, you learn the rest.

Working with Missed and Recent Calls

You can use iPhone's Recents list to get information about the calls you've made with iPhone, well, recently. This includes both calls that were completed and that were missed.

1. On the Home screen, press Phone. You move to the Phone page. At the bottom of the screen, on the Recents button, you see an indicator if you missed any calls since you last looked at the list, along with the number that you missed.

2. Press Recents. The Recents list appears.

3. Press All to see all recent calls, including those you've made, those you've answered, and those you've missed. iPhone highlights calls you missed in red. For each call, you see who made it and the time at which the caller made it.

4. Drag your finger up and down the list to scroll it.

5. To see only missed calls, press Missed. The list reduces to show only missed calls.

6. To return a call, press the contact associated with the call.

7. To get more information about a missed call, press its Info button (if you press the number you'll call it instead). The Info screen appears. Here you see a variety of information about the call, such as who made it, the time at which the caller placed the call, and contact information for the person making the call if that information resides on your contacts list. The number from which the call came shows in blue. You can dial any number shown by pressing it.

8. To return to the Recents list, press Recent Calls.

9. To clear the list, press Clear.

10. Press Clear All Recents. The Recents list is reset.

Adding Caller Information to Favorites

Earlier you learned how simple it is to place calls to someone on your favorites list. There are a number of ways to add people to this list, including adding someone who has called you.

1. On the Home screen, press Phone.

2. Press Recents. The Recents list appears.

3. Press the Info button for the person you want to add to your favorites list. The Info screen appears.

4. Press Add to Favorites. If the person has multiple numbers associated with his contact information, you see each available number.

5. Press the number you want to add as a favorite. You return to the Info screen, and the number is marked with a blue star to show that it is on your favorites list.

6. Repeat step 5 to add the contact's other numbers to the favorites list if you want to.

7. Press Recent Calls. You can call the favorite by pressing the Favorites button and pressing that favorite on the list.

Using iPhone's Headset for Calls

iPhone includes a set of headphones with a microphone on one of its cords. The mic includes a button that you can use to do the following:

- **Answer** Press the mic button once to answer a call.

- **End a call** Press the mic button while you are on a call to end it.

- **Decline a call** Press and hold the mic button for about two seconds. Two beeps sound when you release the button to let you know that iPhone sent the call to voicemail.

- **Put a current call on hold and switch to an incoming call** Press once and then press again.

- **End a current call on hold and switch to an incoming call** Press once and hold for about two seconds. Release the button and you hear two beeps to let you know that you ended the first call. The incoming call is ready for you.

Ringing
When you have headphones plugged into iPhone and you receive a call, the ringtone plays on both the iPhone's speaker and the headphones.

Using Visual Voicemail

Visual voicemail just might be the best of iPhone's many great features. No more wading through long, uninteresting voicemails to get to one in which you are interested. You simply jump to the message you want to hear. And because voicemails are stored on iPhone, you don't need to log in to hear them. If that isn't enough for you, you can also jump to any point within a voicemail to hear just that part.

>>>*step-by-step*

Recording a Greeting

The first time you access voicemail, you are prompted to record a voice-mail greeting. Follow the onscreen instructions to do so. You can also record a new greeting at any time.

1. Move to the Phone screen and press Voicemail. The Voicemail screen appears.

2. Press Greeting. The Greeting screen appears.

3. To use a default greeting that provides only the iPhone's phone number, press default.

4. To record a custom greeting, press Custom. The record tool appears.

5. Press Record. The Recording Personal message appears, and recording begins.

6. Speak your greeting.

Missing Password

If something happens to the password stored on iPhone for your voicemail, such as if you restore iPhone, you are prompted to enter your password before you can access your voicemail. Do so at the prompt and press OK. iPhone logs you in to voicemail, and you won't have to enter your password for a second time unless something happens to it again.

7. When you're done, press Stop. The Play button becomes active.

8. Press Play to hear your greeting.

9. If you aren't satisfied, repeat steps 5 through 8 to record a new message. You can only replace a recorded greeting; you can't change it.

10. When you are happy with your greeting, press Save. iPhone saves the greeting and returns you to the Voicemail screen.

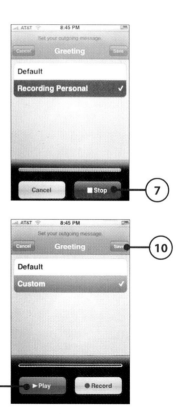

Listening to and Managing Voicemails

Unless you turned off the voicemail sound, you hear a tone each time a caller leaves a voicemail for you. In the Voicemail button on the Phone screen, you also see the number of new voicemails you have. (New is defined as those voicemails to which you haven't listened.)

Number of voicemails
to which you haven't
listened

If you receive a voicemail while iPhone is locked, you see a message on the screen alerting you that iPhone received a voicemail. Drag the slider to the right to jump to the Voicemail screen so that you can work with the message.

New voicemail
has been left.

>>>*step-by-step*

Finding and Listening to Voicemails

1. Move to the Phone screen and press Voicemail. You see the Voicemail screen. The list contains each voicemail you've received. If iPhone recognizes the person who left the message because the number is on your contacts list, it shows the caller's name. If the number isn't recognized, you see the number itself. You also see the time at which the caller left the message. Messages to which you haven't yet listened are marked with a blue dot.

2. Drag up and down the list to scroll the list of voicemails.

3. To listen to a voicemail, press it. It becomes highlighted to let you know that it is the active voice-mail message.

4. Press the message or press its Play button. It begins to play. As it does so, the Playhead moves along the Timeline so that you can see where you are in the message.

5. To hear the message on iPhone's speaker, press Speaker.

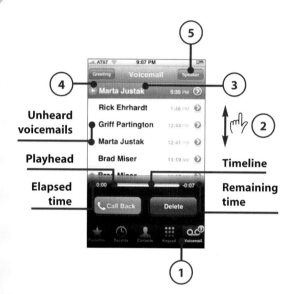

Unheard voicemails

Playhead

Elapsed time

Timeline

Remaining time

6. To pause a message, press its Pause button.

7. To move to a specific point in a message, drag the Playhead to the point at which you want to listen.

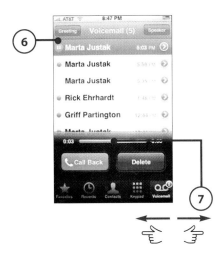

Moving Ahead or Behind

You can also drag the Playhead while a message is playing to rewind or fast-forward it. This is also helpful when you want to listen to specific information without hearing the whole message again.

8. Press the Play button next to the voicemail you want to hear. The message plays from the Playhead's location.

9. To get more information about a message, press its Info button. The Info screen appears. If the person who left the message is on your contacts list, you see her contact information.

10. To return to the Voicemail screen, press Voicemail.

More than Just Information Only

Much of the information on the Info screen is active, meaning that you can press it to do something. For example, to call a listed number, press it. To send an email, press an email address. To visit a website, press its URL.

Two Annoyances of Life Solved

If you deal with lots of voicemails, iPhone solves two annoyances for you. (Well, they're annoyances to me anyway.) The first annoyance involves people who speak too quickly or unclearly when they leave information you need, such as a phone number. With regular voicemail, you have to play the whole message just to hear the information you need. With iPhone, you can drag the Playhead to the point in the message containing the information of interest to hear it as many times as you need.

The other annoyance is dealing with long voicemails. Because iPhone shows you how long each message is, you can decide to listen to a message based on how long it is. And, of course, you see who each message is from, so you can prioritize messages to listen to as you see fit.

>>>*step-by-step*

Deleting Voicemails

1. Move to the Voicemail screen.

2. Press the message you want to delete to select it.

3. Press Delete. iPhone deletes the message, the Deleted Messages option appears, and the next message on the list plays.

Listening to and Managing Deleted Voicemails

1. Move to the Voicemail screen.

2. Scroll down the screen until you see the Deleted Message options.

3. Press Deleted Messages. The Deleted screen appears.

4. Listen to any deleted messages just as you do on the Voicemail screen.

5. To move a message back to the Voicemail screen, select it.

6. Press Undelete. iPhone restores the message to the Voicemail screen.

7. To remove all deleted messages permanently, press Clear All.

8. Press Clear All at the prompt. iPhone erases the deleted messages and returns you to the Deleted screen.

9. To return to the Voicemail screen, press Voicemail.

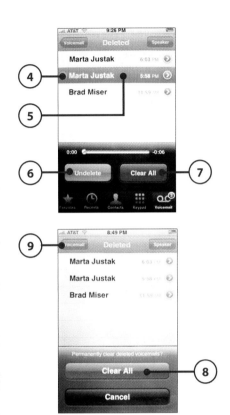

What's Missed

In case you're wondering, iPhone considers any call you didn't answer as a missed call. So if someone calls and leaves a message, that call is included in the counts of both missed calls and new voicemails.

Changing Your Voicemail Password

1. Move to the Settings screen.

2. Press Phone. The Phone screen appears.

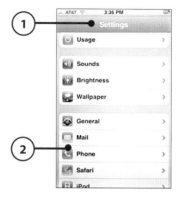

3. Scroll down the screen until Change Voicemail Password appears.

4. Press Change Voicemail Password. The Password screen appears.

5. Enter your current password.

6. Press Done.

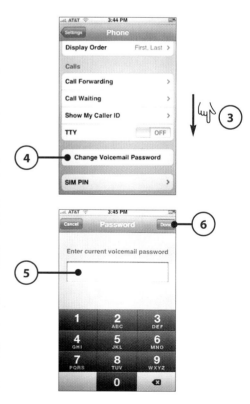

7. Enter the new password.

8. Press Done. The screen refreshes and prompts you to re-enter the new password.

9. Re-enter the new password.

10. Press Done. iPhone saves the new password and returns you to the Phone screen.

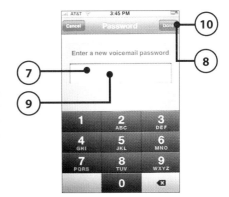

Use Settings to configure how contacts are displayed.

Press here to manage contact information.

In this chapter, you'll learn how to make sure that your iPhone has the contact information you need when you need it. Topics include the following:

→ Configuring how contacts are displayed
→ Getting contact information on iPhone
→ Using contacts on iPhone
→ Changing or deleting contacts

Managing Contacts

Contact information, including names, phone numbers, email addresses, and physical addresses, is vital to getting the most out of iPhone. Because much of iPhone's functionality revolves around interacting with people and organizations, having the information you need for these interactions is critical. Fortunately, you probably have most of the contact information you need already stored on your computer, and you can easily move that information to iPhone. You can also create contacts on iPhone manually and add or refine contact information as you use iPhone.

Configuring How Contacts Are Displayed

Before you start using contacts, make sure that contact information displays according to your preferences.

>>>*step-by-step*

1. On the Home screen, press Settings. The Settings screen appears.

2. Scroll down until you see the Phone settings.

3. Press Phone. The Phone screen appears.

4. Press Sort Order. The Sort Order screen appears.

5. To have contacts sorted by first name and then last name, press First, Last.

6. To have contacts sorted by last name and then first name, press Last, First.

7. Press Phone.

8. Press Display Order. The Display Order screen appears.

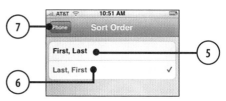

9. To show contacts in the format *first name, last name*, press First, Last.

10. To show contacts in the format *last name, first name*, press Last, First.

11. Press Phone.

Getting Contact Information on iPhone

To be able to use contact information on iPhone, it has to exist there. Fortunately, there are many ways to configure contact information on iPhone.

>>>*step-by-step*

Moving Contacts from a Windows PC to iPhone

If you use Outlook, Windows Address Book/Outlook Express, or Yahoo! Address Book, you can move your contact information from any of those applications onto iPhone.

1. Connect iPhone to your computer.

2. Select iPhone from the Source list.

3. Click the Info tab.

4. Check Sync contacts from.

5. On the pop-up menu, choose the application you use to manage contact information, such as Outlook.

6. To sync all contact information, click All contacts and skip to step 9.

7. If you organize your contact information in groups and want to move only specific ones onto iPhone, click Selected groups.

8. Check the check box next to each group you want to move into iPhone.

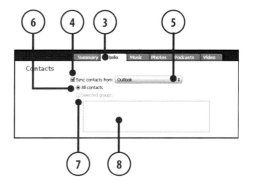

9. Click Apply. The contact information you selected moves onto
iPhone. Each time you sync
iPhone, any changes you make to
the selected contact information
on the PC move onto iPhone, and
changes you make on iPhone
move onto the PC.

Syncing with More than One Source

If you configured iPhone to sync with
more than one source of contact information, perhaps Outlook and Address
Book, when you sync, you're prompted
to replace or merge the information.
If you select Replace Info, the existing
information in whatever you are syncing with replaces all the contact information on iPhone. If you choose Merge
Info, the information you are syncing
moves onto iPhone and merges with
the existing contact information.

Moving Contacts from a Mac to iPhone

If you use Address Book or Yahoo!
Address Book, you can move your
contact information from any of
those applications onto iPhone.

1. Connect iPhone to your Mac.

2. Select iPhone from the Source list.

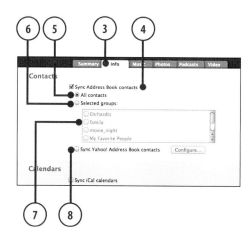

3. Click the Info tab.

4. To sync with Address Book, check Sync Address Book contacts.

5. To sync all contact information, click All contacts and skip to step 9.

6. If you organize your contact information in groups and want to move only specific ones onto iPhone, click Selected groups.

7. Check the check box next to each group you want to move into iPhone and skip to step 9.

8. To sync with Yahoo! Address Book, check Sync Yahoo! Address Book contacts and follow the on-screen prompts to log into your Yahoo! Address Book.

9. Click Apply. The contact information you selected moves onto iPhone. Each time you sync iPhone, any changes you make to the selected contact information on the Mac moves onto iPhone, and changes you make on iPhone move onto the Mac.

Creating New Contacts While Using iPhone

As you use iPhone, you encounter many types of contact information. When you receive phone calls (Chapter 1, "Making, Receiving, and Managing Calls"), you deal with phone numbers. When you send emails (Chapter 5, "Emailing"), you interact with email addresses. If you text message, you use phone numbers (Chapter 7, "Text Messaging"). When you use the Map widget (Chapter 10, "Using Other iPhone Widgets"), you view physical addresses. And these are just examples of some of the places in which you encounter information you might want to use to create a contact. The steps you use to create contacts during any of these activities is similar, as several of the following examples demonstrate.

>>>*step-by-step*

Creating a Contact from a Recent Phone Call

1. On the Home screen, press Phone. The Phone screen appears.

2. Press Recents.

3. Press All to see all recent calls or Missed to see only those calls you didn't answer.

4. Press the Info button for the number from which you want to create a contact. The Info screen appears; the label on the screen depends on the kind of call you select. For example, if you select a missed call, the screen label is Missed Call.

5. Press Create New Contact. The New Contact screen appears. iPhone adds the number you selected and labels it, such as mobile.

6. Use the New Contact screen to configure the new contact. This works just like when you create a new contact manually, except that you already have information for the new contact. See "Creating Contacts on iPhone Manually" later in this chapter for details.

Creating a Contact from an Email

1. On the Home screen, press Mail. The Mail screen appears.

2. Use the Mail application to get to an email (see Chapter 5 for details).

3. Press the email address from which you want to create a new contact. The Info screen appears; the label of the screen depends on the type of email address you pressed. For example, if you pressed the address from which the email was sent, the screen is labeled From.

4. Press Create New Contact. The New Contact screen appears. iPhone adds the email address you selected to the new contact, labeled with iPhone's best guess, such as Home.

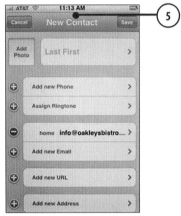

5. Use the New Contact screen to configure the new contact. This works just like when you create a new contact manually, except that you already have information for the new contact. See "Creating Contacts on iPhone Manually" later in this chapter for details.

Creating a Contact from a Text Message Conversation

1. On the Home screen, press Text. The Text Messages screen appears.

2. Move to a text conversation (see Chapter 7 for details).

3. Scroll to the top of the conversation screen.

4. Press Add to Contacts.

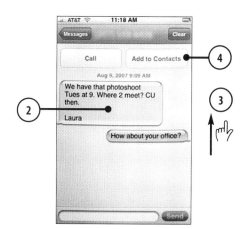

5. Press Create New Contact. The New Contact screen appears. iPhone adds the number you selected and labels it, such as mobile.

6. Use the New Contact screen to configure the new contact. This works just like when you create a new contact manually, except you already have information for the new contact. See "Creating Contacts on iPhone Manually" later in this chapter for details.

Creating a Contact from a Map

1. On the Home screen, press Maps. The Map screen appears.

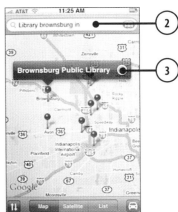

2. Use the map to find a location (Chapter 10 covers the Map widget).

3. Press the Info button for the location. The Info screen appears.

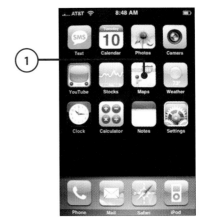

4. Scroll down the screen until you see the Create New Contact button.

5. Press Create New Contact. The New Contact screen appears. iPhone adds as much information as it can based on the location, such as name, phone number, address, website, and so on.

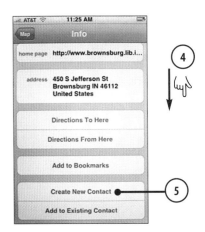

6. Use the New Contact screen to configure the new contact. This works just like when you create a new contact manually, except that you already have information for the new contact. See "Creating Contacts on iPhone Manually," next, for details.

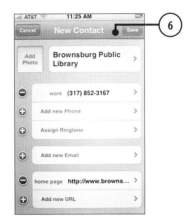

Creating Contacts on iPhone Manually

Most of the time, you'll manage contact information on a computer and move it to iPhone. Or you'll use information on iPhone to create new contacts so that you don't have to start from scratch. When you do have to start from scratch, you can create contacts manually and add all the information you need to them.

1. On the Home screen, press Phone. The Phone screen appears.

2. Press Contacts.

3. Press New Contact. The New Contact screen appears. You see many of the data elements you can include for a contact, such as name, phone numbers, addresses, email addresses, and so on. You can add more fields as needed.

4. To associate a photo with the contact, press Add Photo. The photo dialog appears.

5. To take a photo of the contact, press Take Photo and skip to step 9.

6. To choose an existing photo stored on iPhone, press Choose Existing Photo. The Photo Albums screen appears.

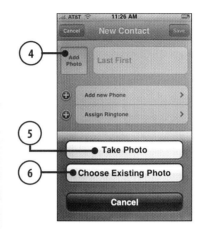

7. Use the Photo Album tools to move to, select, and configure the photo you want to associate with the contact. Chapter 9, "Taking, Storing, and Viewing Photos," covers the details of these steps.

8. Press Set Photo. iPhone configures the photo and saves it to the contact. You return to the New Contact screen and see the photo you selected. Skip to step 12.

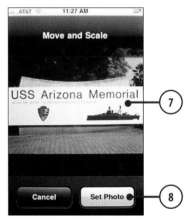

9. Use iPhone camera to capture the photo you want to associate with the contact.

10. Use the Move and Scale screen to configure the photo (Chapter 9 explains this screen).

11. Press Set Photo. iPhone saves the photo, and you return to the New Contact screen.

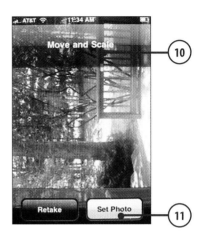

12. Press Last First or First Last (the label you see depends on the preference you set). The Edit Name screen appears.

13. Press the First bar.

14. Enter the first name.

15. Press the Last bar.

16. Enter the last name.

17. Press the Company bar.

18. Enter the company for the contact.

19. Press Save. You return to the New Contact screen and see the information you entered.

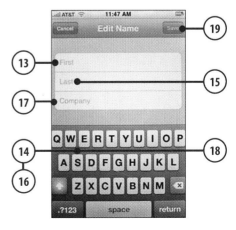

20. Press Add new Phone. The Edit Phone screen appears.

Company Contact

If you're creating a contact for a company or other organization, leave the first and last fields empty. If you don't want to associate a contact with an organization, leave the company field empty.

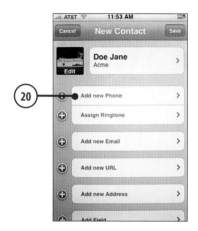

21. Enter the phone number, including area code.

22. Press the label bar. The Label screen appears.

23. Press the label you want to associate with the phone number. You
return to the Edit Phone screen,
and iPhone shows the label you
selected.

24. Press Save. You return to the New
Contact screen and see the number and label you entered.

Custom Labels

You can create custom labels for
various kinds of contact information. On the Label screen, press the
Add Custom Label option. The
Custom Label screen appears.
Create the label and press Save.
You can then choose your custom
label for the new contact you are
creating as well as for contacts you
create or change in the future.

25. To add another number, press
Add new Phone and repeat
steps 21 through 24.

26. To assign a specific ringtone to
play when you receive a call from
the contact, press Assign
Ringtone. The Ringtones screen
appears.

27. Press the ringtone you want to associate with the contact. It plays and iPhone marks it with a check mark to show you that this is the associated ringtone.

28. Press New Contact.

29. Press Add new Email. The Edit Email screen appears.

30. Enter the email address for the contact.

31. Press the label bar. The Label screen appears.

32. Press the label you want to associate with the email address. You return to the Edit Email screen.

33. Press Save.

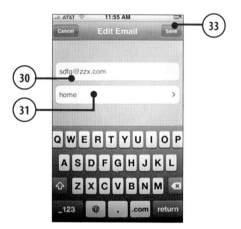

34. To add another email, press Add new Email and repeat steps 30 through 33.

35. To associate a website with the contact, press Add new URL. The Edit URL screen appears.

36. Enter the URL.

37. Press the label bar. The Label screen appears.

38. Press the label you want to associate with the URL. You return to the Edit URL screen.

39. Press Save.

40. To add another URL, press the Add new URL button and repeat steps 36 through 39.

41. Scroll down the screen.

42. To add a new physical address to the contact, press Add new Address. The Edit Address screen appears.

43. If the address is not in the default country shown, such as United States, press the Country button. The Country screen appears.

44. Scroll the screen or use the index to find the country for the address you are creating.

45. Press the country for the address. You return to the Edit Address screen. The data for the address depends on the country you selected. For example, if the country uses state information, you see a State field. If it uses postal codes, you see the Postal Code field.

46. Press the first element of the address, such as Street.

47. Enter the information for that element.

48. Repeat steps 46 and 47 until you've entered all the address's information.

49. Press the label. The Label screen appears.

50. Press the label you want to apply to the address.

51. Press Save.

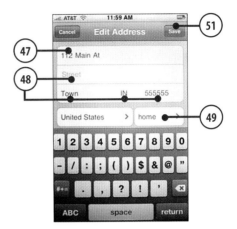

52. To add another address, press Add new Address and repeat steps 43 through 51.

53. To add more fields to the contact, press Add Field. The Add Field screen appears. On this list, you see all possible data that you can add to a contact.

54. Press the data you want to add. The related Edit field appears. For example, if you selected Nickname, the Edit Nickname field appears.

55. Use the Edit screen to enter information for the field you selected. The tools on the Edit screen depend on the kind of information you added.

56. Press Save.

57. To add more fields to the contact, press Add Field and repeat steps 53 through 57.

58. When you finish adding information, press Save.

Using Contacts on iPhone

There are many ways to use contact information. The first step is always finding the contact information you need. Next is to select the action you want to
perform.

1. On the Home screen, press
    Phone. The Phone screen
    appears.

2. Press Contacts. The All Contacts
    screen appears. You see contacts
    listed in the format you selected,
    such as last name, first name.

3. Drag your finger up or down to
    scroll the screen to browse for
    contact information; flick your fin-
    ger up or down to scroll rapidly.

4. Press the index to jump to contact
    information organized by first let-
    ter of the selected format.

5. To view a contact's information,
    press the contact. The Info screen
    appears.

6. Scroll up and down the screen to
    view all the contact's information.

7. Press the data and buttons on the
    screen to perform actions, includ-
    ing the following:

    - **Phone Numbers**   Press a phone
      number to dial it.

    - **Email Addresses**   Press an email
      address to create a new email to it.

    - **URLs**   Press a URL to open Safari
      and move to that website.

    - **Addresses**   Press an address to
      show it in the Map widget.

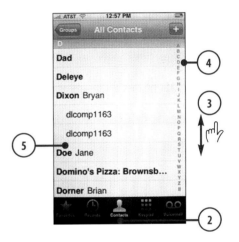

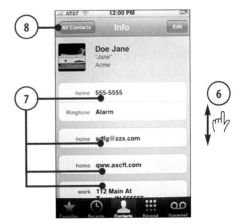

- **Text Message**   Press the Text Message button to send a text message.

- **Add to Favorites**   Press the Add to Favorites button to add the contact information to your Favorites list. When you choose a number, iPhone adds it to your Favorites list and marks it with a blue star to show you that it added the number to the list.

8.   To return to the All Contacts list, press All Contacts.

Changing or Deleting Contacts

Contact information changes as time passes. For example, perhaps you need to add more information to existing contacts, or you don't need contact information anymore; in that case, you can make these changes or remove those contacts from iPhone.

When you sync contacts with a computer, the changes go both ways. For example, when you change a contact on iPhone, the synced contact manager application, such as Outlook, makes the changes for those contacts. Likewise, when you change contact information in a contact manager, those changes move to iPhone when you sync it. If you add a new contact in a contact manager, it moves to iPhone during a sync operation and vice versa.

When you sync, you see a dialog box that prompts you to tell iTunes how to handle the changes made on the computer with which you are syncing.

>>>step-by-step

Changing Contacts via Syncs

1.   Connect iPhone to the computer.

2.   Start the Sync if iTunes doesn't start it automatically. iTunes identifies changes and you see the Sync Alert prompt.

3. To view details, click what you want to see details about, such as Add to see contacts that will be added, Modify to see which contacts will be changed, or Delete to see which contacts will be deleted.

4. To see the details of the contact that will be added, changed, or deleted, click it. Its detail appears.

5. After you review the changes, click Allow to allow the sync to proceed or click Cancel Sync if you don't want to make the changes. If you allow the changes, the contact information in the synced contact manager changes accordingly. If you cancel the sync, iTunes prompts you again the next time you sync. If you don't want the changes ever to be made, you have to undo them on iPhone.

How many contacts will be added

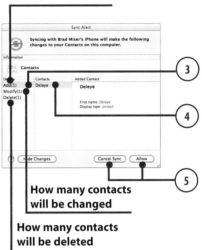

How many contacts will be changed

How many contacts will be deleted

Adding or Removing Information for an Existing Contact Manually

You can change any information for an existing contact on iPhone; when you sync, the changes you make are moved into your contact manager, such as Outlook or Address Book.

1. On the Home screen, press Phone. The Phone screen appears.

2. Press Contacts. The All Contacts screen appears. You see contacts listed in the format you selected, such as *last name, first name*.

3. Drag your finger up or down to scroll the screen to browse for contact information; flick your finger up or down to scroll rapidly.

4. Press the index to jump to contact information organized by first letter of the selected format. For example, if you use the *last name, first name* format, the index is for last names. If you use the *first name, last name* format, the index is for first names.

5. To view a contact's information, press the contact. The Info screen appears.

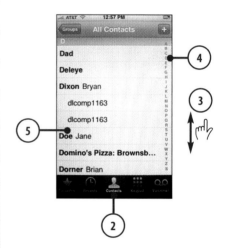

6. Press Edit. The Info screen moves into Edit mode, and you see Unlock and Add buttons.

7. Press a field to change its information. The related Edit screen appears, and you can make or save your changes. These Edit screens work just like when you create a new contact (see "Creating Contacts on iPhone Manually" earlier in this chapter).

8. To add more fields, press the related Add button. These also work just like when you are creating a contact manually.

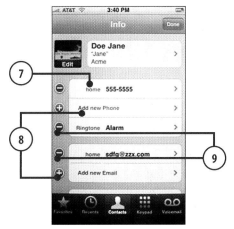

9. To remove a field from the contact, press its Unlock button. The Delete button appears.

10. Press Delete. iPhone removes the field from the contact.

11. When you finish making changes, press Done. iPhone saves the changes, and you return to the Info screen.

Adding Information to an Existing Contact While Using iPhone

As you use iPhone, you'll encounter information related to a contact but that isn't part of that contact's information. For example, a contact might call you on a different phone than the one you entered in that contact's information. When that happens, you can easily add the additional information to an existing contact.

1. Locate the information you want to add to an existing contact, such as a phone number, email address, or website.

2. Press the Info button. The Info screen appears.

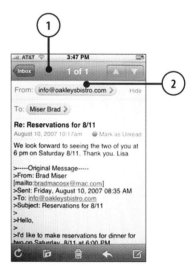

3. Click Add to Existing Contact. The All Contacts screen appears.

Even Easier

In some cases, you don't need to use the Info screen, such as when you are viewing a text message. In those cases, just click the Add to Contact button and choose Add to Existing Contact in the resulting dialog.

4. Locate and press the contact to which you want to add the information. The related Add screen appears depending on the type of information you selected. For example, if you are working with a phone number, the Add Phone screen appears. If you are working with an email address, the Add Email screen appears.

5. Use the Add screen to make changes to the information if needed, such as labeling it. This works just like the Edit screens when you add information for a new contact.

6. Press Save. iPhone adds the information to the existing contact, and you return to wherever you came from, such as an email or text message.

Deleting Contacts Manually

To get rid of contacts, you can delete them from iPhone.

1. Find and view the contact you want to delete.

2. Press Edit.

3. Scroll to the bottom of the Info screen.

4. Press Delete Contact.

5. Press Delete Contact. iPhone deletes the contact and you return to the All Contacts list. The next time you sync, iPhone prompts you to approve the dele-tion on the computer's contact manager, just like other changes you make.

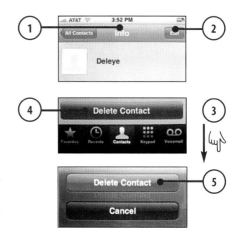

Use to configure iPod functions.

Click to transform iPhone into an iPod.

In this chapter, you'll explore all the iPod functionality that iPhone has to offer. The topics include the following:

→ Stocking iPhone with Audio and Video
→ Listening to music
→ Finding and Listening to podcasts
→ Finding and Watching video
→ Customizing iPhone for iPod

Listening to Audio and Watching Video

One of the best features of iPhone is that in addition to being a telephone, it is also a fully featured iPod you can use to listen to music, podcasts, audiobooks, and other audio content. You can also watch movies, TV shows, and other video on iPhone's large, high-resolution screen. In fact, iPhone's screen is larger and its iPod interface is better than the iPods that were available when iPhone was released. We can expect that all iPods will eventually adopt iPhone's screen and interface because it works so well, which will be a good thing.

It's Not All Good

For the first-generation iPhone, the maximum storage space was 8GB (a 4GB model was also available). Although that's impressive for such a small device, it's not adequate to store all the great content in many people's iTunes libraries, especially when video is involved. The only way to deal with this limitation is to pick and choose the content you want to be available when you are on the move. This isn't hard, but it is a nuisance. Hopefully future versions will include large hard drives, such as the 80GB drive available on the largest iPod when iPhone was first released.

Stocking iPhone with Audio and Video

Before you can listen to audio and watch video on an iPhone, you have to move the content you want to be able to enjoy onto the phone. You do that using iTunes; as you can guess, you need to add content to iTunes before you can move it from iTunes to iPhone. After your iTunes library is chock-full of good stuff, you can easily move that good stuff onto iPhone to enjoy it there.

>>>*step-by-step*

Building Your iTunes Library

The following sections provide the steps to get content in the three most common ways: importing audio CDs, purchasing content from the iTunes Store, and subscribing to podcasts in the iTunes Store.

Importing Audio CDs

Importing audio CDs is one of the most useful ways to get music into iTunes.

1. Launch iTunes by double-clicking its application icon, choosing it on the Windows Start menu, or clicking it on the Mac's Dock.

Only the First Time
You need to only perform steps 2 through 10 before the first time you import CDs or when you want to change settings.

---

2. Choose Edit, Preferences (Windows) or iTunes, Preferences (Mac).

3. Click the Advanced tab.

4. Click the Importing subtab.

5. From the On CD Insert drop-down menu, choose Import CD and Eject.

6. On the Import Using drop-down menu, choose AAC Encoder.

7. On the Setting drop-down menu, choose High Quality.

8. Check Automatically retrieve CD track names from Internet.

9. Check Create filenames with track number.

10. Click OK.

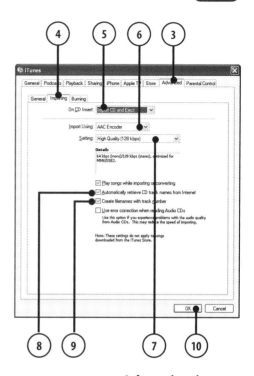

Information about import process

11. Insert a CD into the computer. iTunes connects to the Internet and identifies the CD you just inserted. As soon as that's done, the import process starts. You don't have to do anything because iTunes manages the import process for you. When the process finishes, iTunes ejects the disc.

12. Insert the next CD you want to import. After it has been ejected, insert the next CD and so on until you've added to the iTunes library all the CDs you want to add to iPhone.

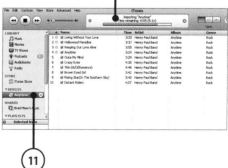

No Duplicates Please

After you import all your CDs, change the iTunes On CD Insert setting to Ask to Import CD so that you don't accidentally import multiple copies of the same CD.

LABELING YOUR MUSIC

To be able to browse and find music in your iTunes library, you must label the songs you import. When iTunes finds a CD's information on the Internet, it takes care of most of this for you. One label that iTunes might not be able to complete for you is the album art associated with the CD. Both iTunes and iPhone show album artwork, so it's a better experience if your music has it.

To have iTunes search for artwork and add it automatically, open the iTunes Preferences dialog box and check Automatically Download Missing Album Artwork. When you click OK, iTunes finds and adds all the artwork it can. You can add art manually by selecting songs and choosing File, Get Info. Click the Artwork tab and use its tools to add graphics to the music.

>>>*step-by-step*

Downloading Audio and Video from the iTunes Store

The iTunes Store has a very large selection of music, movies, TV shows, and other content that you can preview, purchase, and download. To do this, you must have an Apple Store account, also known as an *Apple ID*. You probably already have one because one is required to activate iPhone.

1. Click iTunes Store on the Source
   list. iTunes connects to the iTunes
   Store, and you see the home page.

Already Logged In?

If your Apple ID appears instead of
the Sign In button, you are already
signed in to your iTunes account.

2. Click Sign In. The Sign In dialog
   appears.

3. Enter your Apple ID.

4. Enter your password.

5. Click Sign In. You return to the
   iTunes Store Home page; your
   Apple ID appears in place of the
   Sign In button to show that you
   are signed in.

6. Browse the iTunes Home page
   using the various scroll arrows,
   scroll buttons, and links you see.
   As you move around, you see
   more detail about music you are
   browsing.

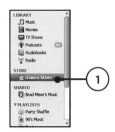

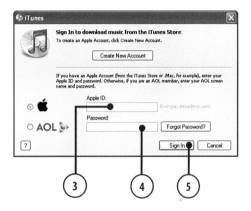

Selected album

7. When you want to purchase and download content, click the Buy button. For example, when you are viewing music, this is the Buy Song or Buy Album button. When you are viewing TV shows, it is the Buy Episode or Buy Season button. The content you purchase is downloaded to your computer and added to your iTunes Library.

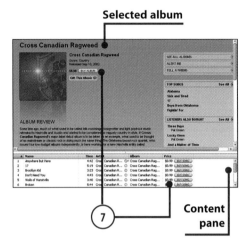

Content pane

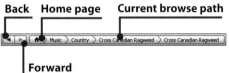

Back Home page Current browse path

Forward

8. Click the Purchased button on the iTunes Source list to see content you've downloaded from the iTunes Store.

Sign Me Up!

If you don't have an Apple ID or want to create a new one, click Create New Account and follow the onscreen instructions.

BUY NOW OR BUY LATER

iTunes enables you to shop with a shopping cart into which all the content you selected gets moved. When you are ready to buy, you move to your shopping cart and check out. You can also buy with one click, meaning that you can click the Buy Now button to immediately purchase or download content.

A preference setting determines which method you use. To configure your iTunes shopping experience, open the Store pane of the iTunes Preferences dialog. When you use the shopping cart, you see the Add button instead of Buy buttons. After you add content to the shopping cart, you select the cart on the iTunes Source list to complete the purchase process.

>>>*step-by-step*

Subscribing to Podcasts in the iTunes Store

Podcasts are radiolike audio segments that you can subscribe and listen to. Even better, most podcasts are free.

1. Click iTunes Store. The iTunes Store fills the Content pane.

2. Click Podcasts. The Podcasts Home page appears.

3. Scroll down until you see the entire Categories section.

4. Click a category you are interested in, such as Technology.

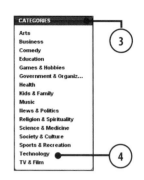

5. Click the Browser button. The browser opens.

6. Click a subcategory in which you are interested.

7. Use the scrollbar in the Content pane to browse all the podcasts available.

8. When you find a podcast you are interested in, select it and click the Play button or just double-click it.

9. When you find a podcast that you would like to try, click its Subscribe button.

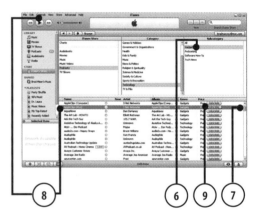

10. Click Subscribe. Under the iTunes Store source, you see the Downloads icon that displays the progress of file downloads, including the number of episodes being downloaded.

11. Click the Podcasts source in the Source list. You see all the podcasts to which you've subscribed.

Building Audio and Video Playlists

One of the best ways to collect content that you want to place on iPhone
is to create a playlist and manually
place content onto it.

1. Click the New Playlist button. A
   new playlist is created with its
   default name selected for you to
   change.

2. Rename the new playlist and press
   Enter (Windows) or Return (Mac).

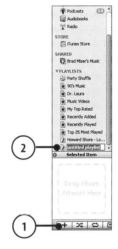

3. Select Music on the iTunes Source
   list.

4. Browse or search for songs you
   want to add to the playlist.

5. Drag songs from the Content
   pane onto the playlist you
   created.

6. Repeat steps 3–5 until you place
   in the playlist all the songs that
   you want it to contain. You can
   place any combination of songs in
   a single playlist.

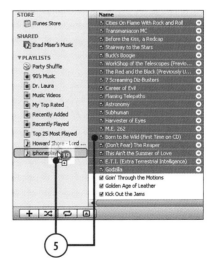

7. Select the playlist. Its contents
   appear in the Content pane.

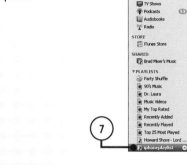

8. Drag songs up and down the
   playlist until they are in the order
   in which you want them to play.

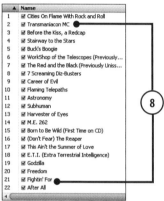

Building Audio and Video Smart Playlists

A smart playlist does the same basic
function as a playlist, which is to collect content that you want to listen to
or watch and to move onto iPhone.
Instead of placing content in a playlist
manually, a smart playlist adds content automatically based on criteria
you define.

1. Select File, New Smart Playlist. The
   Smart Playlist dialog box appears.

2. Select the first tag on which you
   want the smart playlist to be
   based in the Tag menu. For example, you can select the Artist,
   Genre, My Rating, or Year tag,
   among many others.

3. Select the operand you want to use
   on the Operand menu. For example,
   if you want to match data exactly,
   select Is. If you want the condition
   to be looser, select contains.

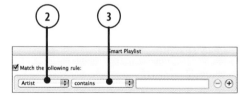

4. Type the condition you want to match in the Condition box. The more you type, the more specific the condition is.

5. To add another condition to the smart playlist, click the Add Condition button. A new, empty condition appears. At the top of the dialog box, the All or Any menu appears.

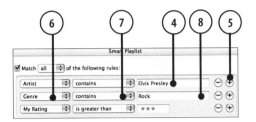

6. Select the second tag on which you want the smart playlist to be based in the second condition's Tag menu.

7. Select the operand you want to use in the Operand menu.

8. Type the condition you want to match from the Condition box.

9. Repeat steps 5–8 to add more conditions to the playlist until you have all the conditions you want to include.

10. Select from the list next to Match at the top of the dialog if all the conditions must be met for a track to be included in the smart playlist or select if only one of them must be met.

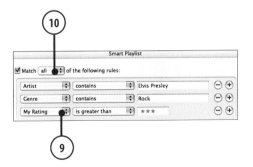

iTunes is Helpful

As you make selections on the Attribute menu and type conditions in the Condition box, iTunes attempts to automatically match what you type to tags in your Library. For example, if your Library includes Elvis music and you use Artist as an attribute, iTunes will enter Elvis Presley in the Condition box for you when you start typing Elvis.

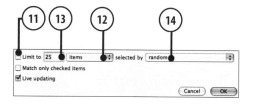

11. If you want to limit the playlist, check the Limit to check box.

12. Select the parameter by which you want to limit the playlist in the first menu; this menu defaults to items. Your choices include the number of items, the time the playlist will play (in minutes or hours), or the size of the files the playlist contains (in MB or GB).

13. Type the data appropriate for the limit you selected in the Limit to box. For example, if you selected minutes in the menu, type the maximum length of the playlist in minutes in the box.

14. Select how you want iTunes to choose the songs it includes based on the limit you selected by using the selected by menu.

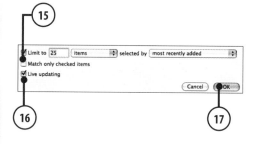

15. If you want the playlist to include only songs whose check box in the Content pane is checked, check the Match only checked items check box.

16. If you want the playlist to be dynamic, meaning that iTunes updates its contents over time, check the Live updating check box. If you uncheck this check box, the playlist includes only those songs that meet the playlist's conditions when you create it.

17. Click OK. You move to the Source list; the smart playlist is added and selected and its name is ready for you to edit. Also, the songs in your library that match the criteria in the playlist are added to it, and the current contents of the playlist are shown.

18. Type the playlist's name and press Enter (Windows) or Return (Mac).

Check Please!

Each item in iTunes has a check box. You use this to tell iTunes if you want it to include the item (such as a song or podcast) in whatever you happen to be doing. If you uncheck this box, iTunes ignores the item.

Moving Audio, Video, and Podcasts onto iPhone

To move iTunes content onto iPhone, you need to choose the content you want to move there and then synchronize iPhone. You can set up iPhone so that content is moved automatically or manually.

1. Insert iPhone into its Dock connected to your computer. iPhone is mounted on your computer and appears in the iTunes Source list.

2. Click the iPhone icon. The iPhone configuration screen appears

3. Click the Summary tab.

4. Check Automatically sync when this iPhone is connected.

5. To prevent items you've unchecked (so that they don't play) in iTunes from being moved to iPhone, check Only sync checked items.

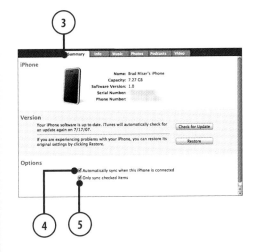

6. Click the Music tab.

7. Check Sync music.

8. Select Selected playlists.

9. Check the check box next to each playlist that you want to move to iPhone.

10. Check Inlcude music videos if you want music videos in your collection to be on iPhone.

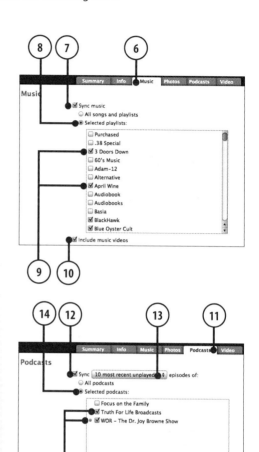

11. Click the Podcasts tab.

12. Check the Sync check box.

13. Choose how many episodes you want to move onto iPhone. Your choice here is limited by the amount of other content you are moving onto iPhone.

14. Select Selected podcasts.

15. Check the check box next to each podcast that you want to move to iPhone.

iTunes Libray Not So Large?

If you have a relatively small amount of content in iTunes, select the All Songs and Playlists option so that iTunes attempts to move all your music onto iPhone. As I mentioned at the start of this chapter, iPhone has limited storage; so, in most cases, you have to choose the content you want to place on iPhone.

16. Click the Video tab.

17. Check the top Sync check box to move TV shows onto iPhone.

18. Choose the number of episodes that should be moved on the pop-up menu. One useful option here is all unwatched, which moves all episodes that you haven't yet watched onto iPhone.

19. Choose the Selected radio button.

20. On the pop-up menu, choose playlists to choose content by playlist or TV shows to choose content by TV series.

21. Check the check box next to each playlist or TV show you want to move to iPhone.

22. Check Sync movies.

23. Check the check box next to each movie you want to move to iPhone.

24. Click Apply. iTunes moves content from its library to iPhone. If you've selected more content than there is room for, you see a warning dialog explaining how much content you selected versus how much is available.

25. Click OK. The dialog closes.

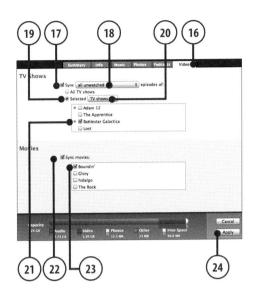

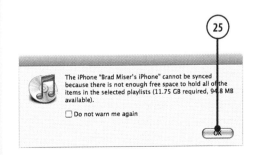

26. Use the information in steps 6–23 to make adjustments to the amount of content you selected.

iPhone's memory usage

Check First, then Unplug

Wait until the Sync Complete message appears in iTunes before removing iPhone from its Dock. If you remove it during the sync process, some of the content might not be moved onto iPhone correctly.

It's Not All Good

Unlike the iPod, there's no way to manually move content onto iPhone. You have to put content into a playlist to be able to move it onto iPhone. This isn't a huge problem, but it can be annoying when there is content you don't want to bother to include in a playlist but want to put on iPhone because it causes a few extra steps for you.

Listening to Music

After you move your tunes to iPhone, you can enjoy them while on the move. There are two fundamental steps to listen to music. First, find the music you want to listen to; from the Cover Flow Browser to artists and genres, iPhone offers many ways to find the tunes you want to hear. Second, after you select your songs, use iPhone's playback controls to listen to your heart's content.

>>>step-by-step

Using the Cover Flow Browser to Find and Play Music

The Cover Flow Browser simulates what it's like to flip through a stack of CDs; you can quickly peruse your entire music collection to get to the right music for your current mood:

1. On the Home screen, press the iPod button.

2. Press one of the music buttons, such as Playlists, Artists, or Songs.

3. Rotate iPhone in the clockwise direction. The Cover Flow Browser appears. Each cover represents an album from which you have at least one song stored on iPhone.

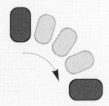

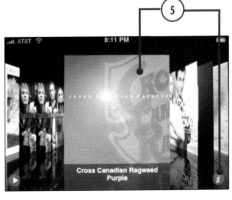

4. To browse your tunes, drag a finger to the right to move ahead in the albums or to the left to move back; the faster you drag, the faster the albums will scroll. Below each cover, you see the name and artist for the album in focus, which is the one that is "face on" to the screen.

5. To see the contents of an album, press its cover or press the Info button when it is in focus. The Contents screen appears showing

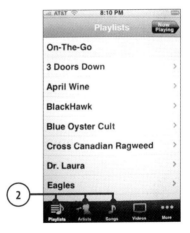

you a list of all the songs on that album. At the top of the screen, you see the album information. Below that, each song is listed along with its playing time.

6. To scroll up or down the list of songs, drag your finger up or down the list of songs.

7. To play a song, press it. The song begins to play. It is marked with a blue arrow, and the Play indicator appears next to the battery icon.

8. To pause a song, press the Pause button. The music pauses, and the Play button replaces the Pause button.

9. To return to the album's cover, press its title information or press the Info button.

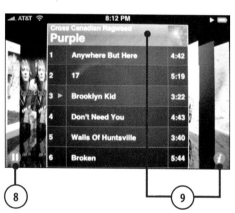

10. While you're listening, you can continue browsing to find more music you want to listen to.

11. Rotate iPhone in the counterclockwise direction to see the Now Playing screen.

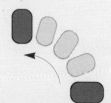

12. Use the Now Playing screen to control the music (covered in detail in the "Playing Music" task later in this section).

Turn It Down! (Or Up!)

No matter which technique you use to find and play music, you can control the volume using the Volume keys on the left side of iPhone.

Using Playlists to Find Music

Accessing the iTunes playlists that you moved to iPhone is simple:

1. On the Home screen, press the iPod button.

2. Press the Playlists button. The list of all playlists on iPhone appears.

Shuffle off to Musical Bliss

To hear the songs in a playlist in random order, press Shuffle. It always appears at the top of a playlist's screen.

3. Press the playlist that you'd like to explore. The list of songs in that playlist appears on a screen with the title of the playlist at the top.

4. Slide your finger up and down the list to see all the songs it contains.

5. To move back to the Playlists screen, press Playlists.

6. When you find the song you want to listen to, press it. The song begins to play, and the Now Playing screen appears.

7. Use the Now Playing screen to control the music (covered in detail in the "Playing Music" section later in this chapter).

8. Press the Return button to move back to the playlist's screen.

Play That Funky Music

The song currently playing is marked with the Speaker icon on the playlist's screen.

Using Artists to Find Music

You can always get to music on iPhone by its artist:

1. On the Home screen, press the iPod button.

2. Press Artists. The list of all artists whose content is on iPhone appears. Artists are grouped by the first letter of their first name or by group name.

3. Slide your finger up and down the list to browse all available artists.

4. To jump to a specific artist, click the letter along the right side of the screen for the artist's last name.

5. Press an artist whose music you'd like to explore. The list of songs by that artist organized by album appears on the Albums screen.

6. Slide your finger up and down the screen to see all the albums for that artist.

7. To see the contents of an album, click it. The list of contents screen appears with the album's title at the top.

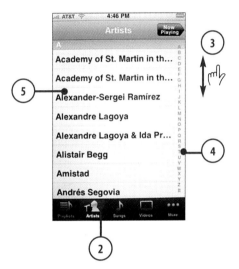

8. Drag your finger up and down the screen to see all the songs on the selected album.

9. To move back to the Albums screen, press Albums.

10. To move back to the Artists screen, press Artists.

Shuffle Music

To hear the songs on an album in random order, press Shuffle. It always appears at the top of the album's screen.

11. Continue browsing artists, albums, and songs until you find songs you want to hear.

12. When you find the song you want to listen to, press it. The song begins to play, and the Now Playing screen appears.

13. Use the Now Playing screen to control the music (covered in detail in the "Playing Music" task later in this section).

14. Press the Return button to move back to the artist's screen.

What's the Speaker Mean?

The song currently playing is marked with the Speaker icon on the album screen.

Using Genres to Find Music

Like the other categories, using Genres to find music is simple:

1. On the Home screen, press the iPod button.

2. Press More. The More screen appears, showing you all the categories of content on iPhone.

3. Press Genres. The Genres screen appears, showing you all the genres of music on iPhone.

4. Slide your finger up and down the list to see all the genres.

5. Press the genre in which you are interested. That genre's screen appears, and you see all the artists whose music is in that genre. At the top of the screen is the All Albums option, which shows you all the albums in that genre on iPhone.

6. When you find an artist whose music you want to view, press it. That artist's screen appears, and you see all the songs by that artist on iPhone, organized by album.

7. Press the genre's button to return to that genre's screen.

8. Continue exploring genres and artists until you find music you want to hear.

9. When you find the song you want to listen to, press it.

10. The song begins to play, and the Now Playing screen appears.

11. Use the Now Playing screen to control the music (covered in detail in the "Playing Music" task later in this section).

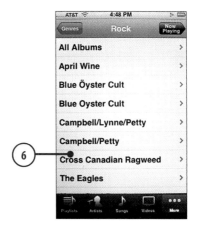

Using the More Menu to Find Music

The More menu shows you all the content categories on iPhone. You can use this menu to access content when it can't be found by one of the category buttons at the bottom of the screen. If you read the previous section, you already know how the More menu works.

1. On the Home screen, press the iPod button.

2. Press More. The More screen appears showing you all the content categories on iPhone.

3. Press the category in which you are interested. That category's screen appears.

4. Browse the category and drill down into its detail to get to songs you want to hear. Browsing categories is similar to browsing playlists, artists, and genres. In fact, these are just three examples of categories available on the More menu.

Playing Music

As you have seen, the Now Playing screen appears whenever you play music. This screen provides several controls for the music and that you use to navigate back to wherever you came from.

1. Find and play a song or album. Now Playing screen appears, and you can use its controls.

2. Press the Track List view button or double-tap the album cover. The album cover view is replaced by the Track List view. Here you see the list of all tracks from which the current song comes, even if you aren't listening to the album itself (such as when you are listening to a playlist). You see the order of tracks on the album along with their names and playing times.

Artist

Song (in bold)

Press to return to the previous screen.

Album art for the album from the currently playing song

Press to return to the start of the current track or press and hold to rewind.

Drag to the right to increase volume or drag to the left to decrease.

Album

Press to skip to the next track or press and hold to fast forward.

Press to pause and then press again to play.

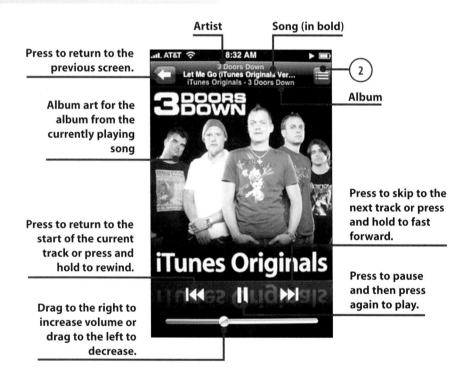

3. Drag your finger up and down to scroll through the tracks in the album.

4. Press a song to play it.

5. Rate the song playing by pressing one of the dots. Stars fill up to the dot you pressed to give the song a star rating between one and five stars.

6. Press the Album button. You return to the Album view.

7. Press the album cover once. The Timeline bar appears.

8. Press the Repeat button once to repeat all the songs in the collection; press it twice to repeat the current song until you stop playback. When the album is set to repeat, the Repeat button turns blue. When the song is set to repeat, the button turns blue and contains a small 1.

9. To move ahead or back in the song, drag the Playhead to the right or left.

10. To play the songs on the album randomly, press the Shuffle button.

11. Press the album cover again. The Timeline bar disappears.

12. Press the Return button. You move back to the screen from which you selected music to play.

13. Press the Now Playing button. You return to the Now Playing screen.

Audiobooks

Another excellent iPod function is the ability to listen to audiobooks. You can get these from the iTunes Store, Audible.com, and many other locations. After you add audiobooks to your iTunes library, you determine whether they are moved to iPhone by using the music-syncing tools. The tools and techniques for listening to audiobooks are just like listening to music.

Viewing Albums

As soon as you play a song from the Track List view screen, you jump to Album mode. From that point on, you are working with the album from which current song came only. For example, if you play a playlist, switch to Track List view, and play a different song on the same album, you change the content to only that album, so the next song that plays is the next one on the album, not the next one in the playlist. When you press the Return button, you move to the album's screen instead of the playlist's screen. If you view only the song's information or give it a rating in Track List view, when you move back to the Cover view, you are still working with the original source, such as a playlist.

Finding and Listening to Podcasts

iPhone is a great way to listen to your podcasts. Like all other iPod functions, you first find the podcast you want to listen to and then use iPhone's audio playback controls to hear it.

>>>step-by-step

1. On the Home screen, press the iPod button.

2. Press the More button. The More screen appears showing you all the content categories on iPhone.

3. Press Podcasts. The Podcasts screen appears showing you the podcasts to which you are subscribed and that have been moved onto iPhone.

4. Press the podcast to which you want to listen. The list of episodes for that podcast is shown; the name of the list screen is the name of the podcast. Podcasts to which you haven't listened are marked with a blue dot.

5. Press the episode you want to hear. The podcast begins to play, and the Now Playing screen appears.

6. To control the podcast, use the controls on the Now Playing screen, which work just as they do when you are playing music. (See the previous section for details.)

Finding and Watching Video

iPhone is a great way to enjoy video content, such as movies or TV shows, while you're on the move. Like music and other content, the first step is to find the video you want to watch. Then you use iPhone's video tools to watch that video.

>>>*step-by-step*

Finding Video

Finding video content on iPhone is the same as finding the other kinds of content we've already discussed:

1. On the Home screen, press the iPod button.

Going Back Again

When content is playing and you press the iPod button, you move to the Now Playing screen. To get back to the iPod screen, press the Return button until the iPod buttons appear at the bottom of the screen.

2. Press Videos. The Videos screen appears showing you the video content on iPhone.

3. To watch a movie or music video, press it. The screen rotates, and the content begins to play; see the next section for details of controlling video.

4. To watch a TV show, click the series you want to watch. A list of available episodes appears. Episodes you haven't watched are marked with a blue dot.

5. Press the episode you want to watch. The screen rotates, and the episode begins to play; see the next section for details of controlling video.

Press to return to the Videos screen.

Watching Video

When you play video, it is always oriented in landscape mode so that it can fill the screen.

1. Press the video. The video controls appear.

Elapsed time

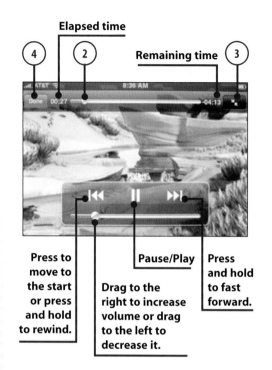

2. Drag the playhead to the right to move ahead or to the left to move backward.

3. Press the Scale button to scale the video to fit the screen or to show it in its native scale. After a few seconds, the video controls disappear.

Scale This

If native scale of the video is not the same proportion as the iPhone screen and you play it in its original scale, the video might not fill the screen. When you scale the video, it fills the screen, but some content might be cut off.

4. When you're done watching, press Done. You move back to the Videos screen.

Remember Where You Were?

For most kinds of video, iPhone remembers where you left off. So if you stop a movie somewhere in the middle, when you restart it, iPhone picks up where you left off.

Deleting Video

Because it takes up a lot of space, video is the only content you can delete from iPhone. There are two ways to delete video content.

When a video finishes, a prompt appears enabling you to keep the video on iPhone or delete it. You can also delete video at any time.

1. Move to the Videos screen.

2. Drag left or right on the video you want to delete. The Delete button appears.

3. Press Delete. A warning prompt appears.

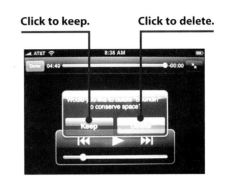

Click to keep.   Click to delete.

4. Press Delete again to delete the video or Cancel to keep it. When video content is deleted from iPhone, it remains in your iTunes library, so you can always move it back onto iPhone at a later time.

Music Video Without the Video

If you want to hear the audio from a video without watching it, choose it from any screen except the Videos screen. Only its audio content plays.

Customizing iPhone for iPod

You could use iPhone as an iPod just fine without performing any of the steps in this section. However, because this book is named *My iPhone*, you should explore these options to make iPhone your own.

Building and Editing an On-The-Go Playlist

You can build a special playlist on iPhone. This is called the On-The-Go playlist because, well, you build it while you are on the go.

Creating and Listening to an On-The-Go Playlist

1. Move to the Playlists screen.

2. Press On-The-Go. The Songs screen appears.

Add from Anywhere

While you're in Playlist-building mode, you can add content from any iPod screen. For example, to add content by artist instead of by song, press the Artists button. The Artists screen appears. Press the artist whose music you want to add to the playlist and add the songs by that artist by pressing those songs or clicking the Add buttons. You can add content by genre, composer, and so on in the same way.

3. Drag your finger up and down the screen to browse all the songs on iPhone.

4. To add a song to the playlist, press the song or the Add button. After you add a song, it is grayed out to show it's already part of the playlist. You can add the same song to the playlist only one time.

5. Repeat steps 3 and 4 until you've added all the songs that you want the playlist to contain.

6. Press Done. You move to the On-The-Go playlist screen and see the songs it contains.

7. Play the On-The-Go playlist just like playlists you've moved from the iTunes library.

All at Once
You can add all the songs shown on any screen by pressing Add All Songs.

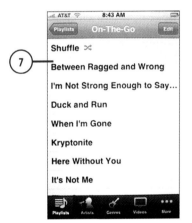

>>>*step-by-step*

Changing an On-The-Go Playlist

1. Move to the Playlists screen and press the On-The-Go playlist. You see the On-The-Go playlist screen.

2. Press Edit. The screen changes to edit mode.

Clear It

To remove all songs from a playlist, press Clear Playlist and then press Clear Playlist again. The playlist is returned to an empty state.

3. To add songs, press the Add button; this works just like when you added songs to the playlist originally. (See the previous section for details.)

4. When you're done adding songs, press Done. You return to the On-The-Go playlist screen.

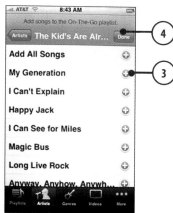

5. To change the order in which songs play, press the List button and drag a song to its new position on the playlist.

6. To remove songs, press the Unlock button. The Delete button appears.

7. Press Delete. The song is removed from the playlist.

8. When you're finished making changes, press Done. You move back to the On-The-Go playlist screen.

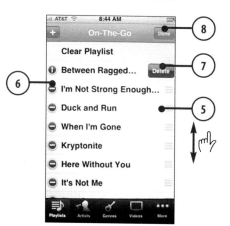

>>> Go Further

SAVING THE ON-THE-GO PLAYLIST

When you sync iPhone, the On-The-Go playlist moves into your iTunes library where you can work with it just like playlists you create in iTunes. For example, you can change its name, its content, and so on.

Each time you change the On-The-Go playlist on iPhone, a new version is created. When you sync, that version moves into iTunes, and its name is updated with a sequential number, as is On-The-Go1, On-The-Go2, and so on. Each version becomes a new playlist in your iTunes library.

Configuring iPhone's iPod Toolbar

The four buttons at the bottom of the iPod screen enable you to get to specific content quickly. You can choose three of the buttons that appear on the screen to make accessing content by that type even easier and faster.

1. Move to the More screen.

2. Press Edit. The Configure screen appears.

3. Drag the button you want to add
to the toolbar to the location of
one of the buttons currently
there. As you get over the current
button, it lights up to show you
that it will be the one replaced
when you lift your finger. The
button you dragged replaces the
button over which you placed it.
The original button is moved
onto the Configure screen.

4. Repeat step 3 until the four buttons you want to be on the toolbar are there. (The fifth button is
always the More button.)

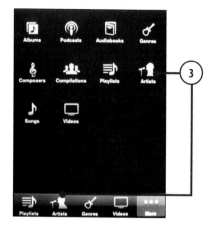

More, Always More

You can't replace the More button. It always appears on the iPod
toolbar.

5. Press the Done button located in
the upper-right corner of the
screen. The iPod toolbar contains
the buttons you placed on it
along with the More button.

Configuring iPhone's iPod Settings

There are few iPod settings you use to configure various aspects of iPhone's iPod functionality:

1. Press the Home button to move back to iPhone's Home.

2. Press Settings. The Settings screen appears.

3. Scroll down until you see the iPod settings option.

4. Press iPod. The iPod Settings screen appears.

5. Press Sound Check if you want iPhone to attempt to even the volume of the music you play so that all the songs play at about the same relative volume level. Press Sound Check to turn it off again; the current status is indicated by the ON or OFF button being available. (If ON is shown, Sound Check is off.)

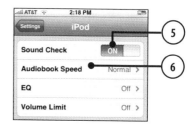

6. To set the speed at which audiobooks play, press Audiobook Speed. The Audiobook Speed screen appears.

7. Press the speed at which you want audiobooks to play; the current speed is indicated by the check mark.

8. Press iPod.

9. To set an equalizer, press EQ. The EQ screen appears.

10. Select the equalizer you want iPhone to use when you play music; the current equalizer is indicated by the check mark. To turn the equalizer off, select Off.

11. Press iPod.

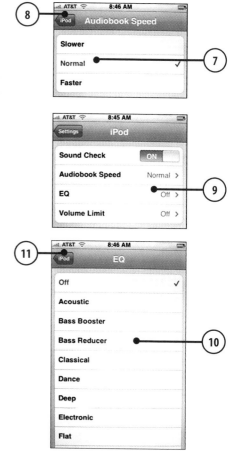

12. To set a limit to the volume level on iPhone, press Volume Limit. The Volume Level screen appears.

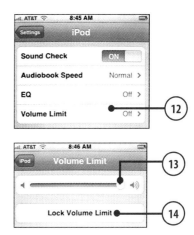

13. Drag the volume slider to the point that you want the maximum volume level to be.

14. To lock this control so that it can't be changed without a passcode, press Lock Volume Limit. The Set Code screen appears.

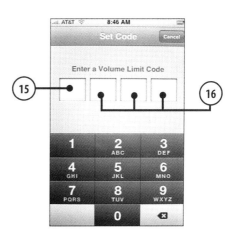

15. Press a digit, which becomes the first digit in the code.

16. Press each of the other three digits to create a four-digit code.

17. Re-enter the code to confirm it. If the code matches, you return to the Volume Limit screen, and the code is set.

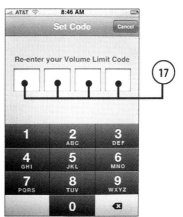

18. To make changes to a locked volume limit, press Unlock Volume Limit.

19. Enter the code. The volume limit is unlocked, and you can change it again.

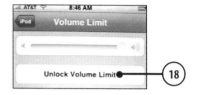

Forgot the Code?

If you forget the passcode, you can reset or restore iPhone to clear it. See Chapter 12, "Maintaining iPhone and Solving iPhone Problems," to learn how.

Go here to connect iPhone to the Internet, Bluetooth devices, and VPN networks.

In this chapter, you'll explore how to connect iPhone to networks and devices. Topics include the following:

→ Connecting to the Internet
→ Connecting to Bluetooth devices
→ Connecting to VPNs

Connecting to the Internet, Bluetooth Devices, and VPNs

Even if you've read this book in sequential order, you know that iPhone is unlike any other personal digital device. If all it contained were the cell phone and iPod functionality, it would still be amazing. However, iPhone is just getting started. It really begins to shine when you use its Internet functions, such as email, web browsing, maps, weather, and…well, you get the idea. As you can probably guess, to use iPhone's Internet functions, you have to connect it to the Internet. You might also want to connect iPhone to Bluetooth devices, such as a Bluetooth headset. Or you might want to connect iPhone to a virtual private network (VPN) so that you can use it to access the resources available on that network. This chapter teaches you the techniques for accomplishing all of that and more.

Connecting to the Internet

When it comes to connecting iPhone to the Internet, you have two options. One is to connect via a Wi-Fi broadband connection that is very, very good, and you'll enjoy the iPhone's Internet functionality at amazing speeds. The other is through AT&T's EDGE network that is so slow you might not be able to stand it for some functions, such as web browsing; still, there are some situations in which connecting, even at a snail's pace, is useful.

It's Not All Good

Unfortunately, for whatever reasons, AT&T and Apple elected to connect iPhone to AT&T's EDGE network by default. Although the EDGE network is widely available, it is not a high-speed connection to the Internet. The first time you try to browse a web page on EDGE, you'll be on edge because it's so slow. It's frustrating because AT&T does have a high-speed Wi-Fi network (G3) that would have been a much better partner with iPhone's amazing Internet functionality. I'm sure there were good reasons for going with EDGE instead, but I hope that at some point, iPhones switch over to the G3 network so that we aren't saddled with EDGE when Wi-Fi isn't available.

The workaround to this is to have access to a Wi-Fi network. The good news is that most public places such as airports, coffee shops, and such have Wi-Fi networks available. The bad news is that sometimes you have to pay to access those networks, and not all of them are available in all locations. Even if you subscribe to a Wi-Fi service for iPhone, you still might have to suffer with the EDGE network from time to time.

Connecting to the Internet via Wi-Fi Networks

You can connect iPhone to a variety of Wi-Fi networks, including those available in public places, such as airports and schools. And you might have a Wi-Fi network in your home. Even though finding a network that you can use (especially at no cost) can be a challenge, connecting to available networks is certainly not.

Automatic Prompting to Join

By default, when you access one of iPhone's Internet functions, such as Safari, iPhone automatically searches for networks to join if you aren't already connected to one. A dialog appears showing you all the networks available to you. You can select and join one of these networks similar to how you join one via Settings, as you learn how to do in the following steps. If you don't want iPhone to do this, move to the Wi-Fi Networks screen and turn off Ask to Join Networks. When it's off, you need to connect to networks each time you want to join using the Settings controls as described in the following steps.

>>>*step-by-step*

Connecting to a Broadcast Network

Many Wi-Fi networks broadcast their information so that you can easily see them when searching with iPhone. These are the easiest to join.

Some networks charge access fees; in these situations, you need a username and password to be able to access the Internet over the network. Without a username and password, you can connect to the network, but you'll be able to access only the provider's login page that you can use to log in or obtain an account.

1. On the Home screen, press Settings. The Settings screen appears.

2. Press Wi-Fi.

3. If Wi-Fi is turned off, press the OFF button to turn it on. Wi-Fi status becomes ON, and iPhone immediately starts searching for available networks.

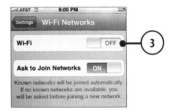

Network name

4. Review the networks that iPhone finds.

5. Press the network you want to join. If you recognize only one of the networks, you probably used it before, and so it is a good choice. You also need to check the security of the network; if you see the lock icon, you need a password to join the network, and you have to do the following two steps. If the network is not marked with the lock icon, it is an open network, and you can skip the following two steps. Finally, look at the signal strength; a stronger signal (more waves) is better. If you select a network that requires a password, the Enter Password screen appears.

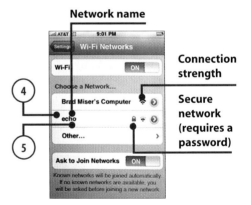

Connection strength

Secure network (requires a password)

6. Press Security. There are different kinds of passwords, including WEP and WEP hex or ASCII. You need to make sure that you are entering the correct kind of password for the network. If the information is for a network that you didn't set up, you should have received the type of password, too. If you set up the network, you should know the kind of security it uses. A check mark indicates the current password type.

7. Press the type of password you have to enter.

8. Press Enter Password.

9. Enter the password for the network.

10. Press Join. iPhone attempts to connect to the network. If you provide the correct password, iPhone connects to the network and gets the information it needs, such as an IP address. If not, you're prompted to enter the password again. After you connect to the network, you return to the Wi-Fi screen.

11. Review the network information. The network to which you are connected is in blue and is marked with a check mark. You continue to see the signal strength for that network.

12. Press the Info button for the network to which you are connected. You see the Info screen, labeled with the name of the network.

13. Scroll the screen to review the network's information. The most important item is the IP Address. If there is no number here or the number starts with 169, the network is not providing an IP address, and you must find another network. You can safely ignore the rest of the information on the screen in most situations. If you want to access some of the more advanced settings, such as HTTP proxy, you need information from the network administrator to be able to access the network, so you need help to get iPhone connected.

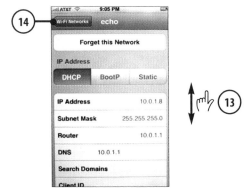

14. Press Wi-Fi Networks to return to the Wi-Fi Networks screen.

Was Connected but Now I'm Not

If you've been using a network successfully, and at some point, iPhone cannot access the Internet but remains connected to the network, move to the network's Info screen and press Renew Lease. This sometimes refreshes iPhone's IP address so that you can access the Internet again.

Wi-Fi connection

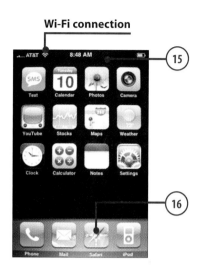

15. Move to the Home screen. You should see the Wi-Fi connection icon next to AT&T. If you see an E instead, you're connected to the EDGE network, meaning that you didn't connect to the network successfully. Repeat the previous steps or try switching networks.

16. Press Safari. Safari opens.

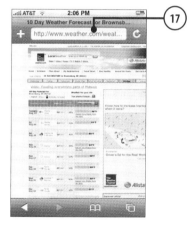

17. Try to move to a web page. (See Chapter 6, "Surfing the Web," for details.) If you move to a web page that is not from a Wi-Fi provider, you're good to go and can start relishing your high-speed bliss. If you are taken to a web page for a Wi-Fi provider, you need an account to be able to access the network. If you have a username and password for the network, enter them on the login form. If you don't have an account, you must obtain one; use the web page to sign up. After you have an account, you can get to the Internet.

Security Key Index

Some private networks require a key index in addition to a password. Unfortunately, there's no way to enter a specific key on iPhone. If a network requires this key, you can't connect iPhone to it. You might even be able to join the network, but you probably won't be able to get an IP address from it, and you must have one to get to the Internet. If you are unable to join a Wi-Fi that you know is available, check with the administrator to make sure that you have the right configuration information and don't need a key index.

Connecting to a "Hidden" Network

Some networks don't broadcast their names or availability. In those cases, you must know the network's name to be able to connect to it because it won't show up on the network list. You also need to know what kind of security the network uses and the password you need to use. You have to get this information from the network's administrator.

1. On the Home screen, press Settings. The Settings screen appears.

Be Known

After iPhone connects to a network (broadcast or hidden) successfully, it becomes a known network. iPhone automatically connects to known networks when it needs to access the Internet. So, unless you tell iPhone to forget about a network, you need to log in to it only the first time.

2. Press Wi-Fi.

3. If Wi-Fi is turned off, press the OFF button to turn it on. Wi-Fi status becomes ON, and iPhone immediately starts searching for available networks.

4. Press Other. The Other Network screen appears.

5. Enter the name of the network.

6. Press Security. The Security screen appears.

7. Press the type of security the network uses. The options are WEP, WEP hex or ASCI, WPA, or WPA2. You don't need to worry about what each of these options means; you just need to pick the right one for the network. (The None option is for unsecured networks, but it's unlikely that a hidden network wouldn't require a password.)

8. Press Other Network. You move back to the Security screen. The Password field appears.

9. Enter the password.

10. Press Join. If the information you entered matches what the network requires, you join the network and can begin to access its resources. If not, you see an error message and have to try it again until you are able to join. When you join the network, you move back to the Wi-Fi screen.

WIFI connection

11. Move to the Home screen. You should see the Wi-Fi connection icon next to AT&T. If you see an E instead, you're connected to the EDGE network, meaning that you didn't connect to the network successfully. Repeat the previous steps or try switching networks.

12. Press Safari. Safari opens.

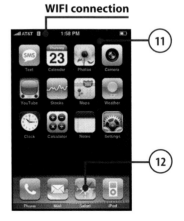

13. Try to move to a web page. (See Chapter 6 for details.) If you move to a web page that is not from a Wi-Fi provider, you're good to go and can start relishing your high-speed bliss. If you are taken to a web page for a Wi-Fi provider, you need an account to be able to access the network. If you have a username and password for the network, enter them on the login form. If you don't have an account, you must obtain one; use the web page to sign up. After you have an account, you can get to the Internet.

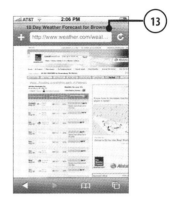

Changing Networks

You can change the network that iPhone is using at any time. For example, if you lose Internet connectivity on the current network, you can move iPhone onto a different one.

1. On the Home screen, press Settings. The Settings screen appears. The network to which iPhone is currently connected is shown.

2. Press Wi-Fi. iPhone scans for available networks and presents them to you in the Choose a Network section of the Wi-Fi Networks screen.

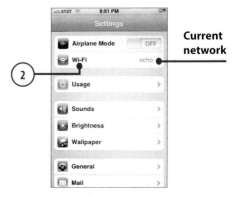

Current network

3. Press the network that you want
    to use. iPhone attempts to join
    the network. If you haven't joined
    that network previously and it
    requires a password, enter it when
    prompted to do so. After iPhone
    connects, you see the new net-
    work's name highlighted in blue
    and marked with a check mark.

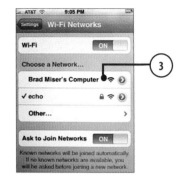

Forgetting Networks

As you learned earlier, iPhone
remembers networks you have
joined and connects to them automatically as needed. Although this is
mostly a good thing, occasionally
you won't want to use a particular
network any more. You might want
iPhone to forget about that network
so that it doesn't automatically use it
in the future.

1. On the Home screen, press
    Settings. The Settings screen
    appears. The network to which
    iPhone is currently connected is
    shown.

2. Press Wi-Fi.

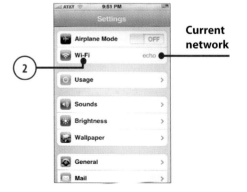

**Current
network**

3. Press the Info button for the network that you want iPhone to forget. That network's Info screen
appears.

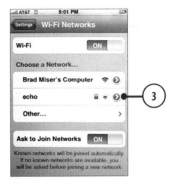

4. Press Forget this Network.

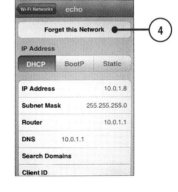

5. Press Forget Network in the
resulting prompt. iPhone forgets
the network, and you return to
the Info screen.

6. Press Wi-Fi Networks. You return
to the Wi-Fi Networks screen. If a
network you've forgotten is still
available to iPhone, it continues to
appear in the Choose a Network
list, but iPhone won't automatically connect to it. You can rejoin the
forgotten network at any time just
as you did the first time you connected to it.

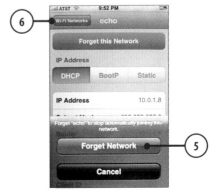

NETWORKING COMPLEXITIES

The good news is that connecting to networks with iPhone is simple, at least most of the time. In some situations, especially non-publicly accessible networks within businesses, you won't be able to use the standard settings, such as DHCP, for most public (and private for that matter) networks. (DHCP stands for *Dynamic Host Configuration Protocol* in case you are wondering.)

If you need to access a network via BootP or static addressing, you'll likely need some help, especially to get the information you need to connect to networks using these methods. After you have that information, you can use the Info screen to enter it as needed. Doing so is beyond the scope of this book, but some quick Net searches will help you understand some of the terminology. Mostly it's a matter of plugging the right information provided to you in the right places.

Connecting to the Internet via EDGE

To connect to AT&T's low-speed network, you don't really need to do anything because iPhone connects to it by default when it can't join a Wi-Fi network. iPhone always prompts you to join a Wi-Fi network when at least one is available. If no Wi-Fi networks are available or you can't join the ones that are, iPhone connects to the EDGE network automatically so that you can still use iPhone's Internet functionality. Unfortunately, the speed is so slow that you'll need much more patience than I have to use the Web. The EDGE network can work okay for email and some of the other less data-intensive functions, however.

Making the EDGE Bearable

You can use Google's proxy server to make surfing the web faster when you are on the EDGE network. While it is faster, the pages you see are formatted for mobile phones, and they don't look much like standard web pages. Still, at least you can actually use the information because it's loaded in a reasonable amount of time. To do this, open Safari and move to www.google.com/m (the "m" is for mobile). View the page in the Mobile mode by clicking the Mobile link. Then click Settings. Set the Format web pages for your phone option to On and click Save. Now when you browse, you get much better performance, although you see pages formatted for mobile phones. This works as long as you move to pages through the Google site. If you move directly to web pages without going through Google, then you'll experience normal EDGE performance and webpage formatting.

EDGE network

When iPhone connects to the EDGE network, you see the E icon.

While you are using the EDGE for Internet functions, cell phone functionality might be disrupted.

Airplane Mode

The exception to iPhone always connecting to at least the EDGE network is when iPhone is in Airplane mode. In this mode, iPhone can't transmit or receive information, including over an Internet connection.

Connecting to Bluetooth Devices

iPhone includes built-in Bluetooth support so that you can use this wireless technology to connect to other Bluetooth-capable devices. The most likely device to connect to iPhone in this way is a Bluetooth headset, but there might be times when you connect other devices to iPhone, too. Connecting any device to iPhone using Bluetooth is similar to the following steps that demonstrate how to connect iPhone to a standard Bluetooth earpiece for hands-free cell phone calls.

>>>*step-by-step*

1. On the Home screen, press Settings. The Settings screen appears.

2. Press General. The General screen appears.

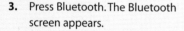

3. Press Bluetooth. The Bluetooth screen appears.

4. Press OFF. Bluetooth starts up, and the status becomes ON. iPhone immediately begins searching for Bluetooth devices.

5. Turn on the Bluetooth headset. The two devices find each other. On iPhone, the headset is listed but shown as not paired.

6. Press the name of the headset to pair it. The Enter PIN screen appears.

7. Enter the device's PIN. This number should be included in the documentation that came with the device.

8. Press Connect. iPhone starts communicating with the device, and you return to the Bluetooth screen. The devices to which iPhone is connected are shown in the Devices list. When iPhone and another device are communicating successfully, the Devices list shows them as paired.

9. Press General. You're ready to use the Bluetooth headset.

When you make a call, iPhone prompts you to use the Bluetooth headset. Press the headset you want to use; if you don't choose, iPhone uses whichever device is marked with the speaker icon that indicates the default device.

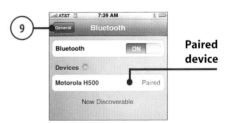

Paired device

Bluetooth headset is the default.

It Takes Two to Pair

In Bluetooth, *pairing* is the lingo for two Bluetooth devices connecting. This requires two things. One is that the devices can communicate with each other via Bluetooth. The other is a pairing code or PIN. Sometimes you enter this code on both devices or, as you saw in the headset example, you enter one device's code on the other device.

Connecting to VPNs

Many organizations use a VPN to provide access to a local network from devices outside that network. For example, many businesses enable employees to connect to internal resources from outside their local networks so that those employees can have access to the same resources they do when they are "on the inside." You can connect to VPNs on iPhone as well.

To connect to a VPN, you must know specific information about how to connect and the various settings you have to enter to be able to connect. You must obtain this information from the network's administrator. After you have that information, you can configure iPhone to connect to the VPN.

>>>*step-by-step*

1. On the Home screen, press Settings. The Settings screen appears.

2. Press General. The General screen appears.

3. Press Network. The Network screen appears.

4. Press VPN. The VPN screen appears.

5. Press OFF. The VPN status becomes ON, and the account settings screen appears.

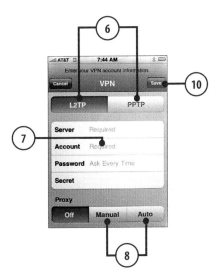

6. Press L2TP or PPTP.

7. Enter the required information in each field, including server, account, password, and secret.

8. If the VPN uses a proxy server, press Manual or Auto.

9. If you pressed Manual, enter the proxy information.

10. Press Save. If the information you entered is correct, iPhone connects to the VPN.

Press to
configure
email
accounts
and
settings.

Press to
use
email.

In this chapter, you'll explore all the email functionality that iPhone has to offer. Topics include the following:

→ Configuring email accounts on iPhone
→ Configuring global email settings
→ Working with email
→ Managing email accounts

Emailing

For most of us, email is an important way we communicate with others, both in professional and personal life. Fortunately, iPhone has great email tools so that you can work with email no matter where you are. You can read, send, reply, and do all the other email actions you might expect from the comfort and convenience of your iPhone.

You can configure multiple email accounts on iPhone so that you can access all of them there. Even better, you can sync iPhone's email accounts with your computer so that adding email accounts to iPhone is effortless.

Get Connected

To use email, you must have an Internet connection. Unlike web browsing and some other Internet functionality, the EDGE network is fast enough for email as long as you don't have too many large messages and are a bit patient. But you'll get the best results using Wi-Fi. To learn how to connect iPhone to the Internet, see Chapter 4, "Connecting to the Internet, Bluetooth Devices, and VPNs."

Configuring Email Accounts on iPhone

Before you can start using iPhone for email, you have to configure the email accounts you want to access with it. iPhone supports a number of email services including Yahoo!, GMail, .Mac, and AOL. You can also configure any email account that uses POP (Post Office Protocol and no, I'm not making that up) or IMAP (Internet Message Access Protocol); this is good because almost all email accounts provided through ISPs (Internet service providers) use one of these two formats. You can also configure email delivered through an Exchange server as long as it supports IMAP.

It's Not All Good

One of the worst failings of iPhone is that it doesn't support email through many Exchange servers by default. That's bad because many businesses and other organizations use Exchange servers for email and most don't allow IMAP access, which you have to be able to use to get email on iPhone. Many organizations do allow web access to email through an OWA (Outlook Web Access) server, but unfortunately, iPhone's current version of Safari is incompatible with that functionality, so that doesn't help.

There are two workarounds for this problem. One is to set up email to automatically forward from the Exchange account to an account you can access on iPhone when you aren't able to access the computer you use for Exchange email. This works and doesn't cost you anything, but it's a bit klunky because when you reply, you have to change the address to be the sender's (it is yours by default because you reply to the forwarded messages), and any replies you send come from the account you forwarded the email to instead of the Exchange email account.

The other workarounds require additional software or fees but work better. Shortly after iPhone was released, several options were released, and more are expected because getting email from Exchange servers is so important for business users of iPhone. See "Configuring Email Accounts for Exchange Servers That Don't Support IMAP," later in this chapter for the details of implementing one of these solutions. You can also do a web search for "Exchange email on iPhone" to see what's available at the time you are reading this.

Syncing Email Accounts with a Windows PC

You can sync email accounts from Outlook or Outlook Express on a Windows PC with iPhone to quickly configure it to work with email for those accounts.

1. Connect iPhone to your computer.

2. Select iPhone from the Source list in iTunes.

3. Click the Info tab.

4. Scroll down until you see the Mail Accounts section.

5. Check Sync selected mail accounts from.

6. On the pop-up menu, choose the email application configured with the accounts you want to move onto iPhone.

7. Check the check box for each account you want to move onto iPhone. You can choose to move any or all of your email accounts in the selected application to iPhone.

8. If you want the email accounts to replace the accounts currently on iPhone, check Mail Accounts; if you leave this unchecked, the selected email accounts are added to iPhone, leaving those already configured on it unchanged.

9. Click Apply. The sync process runs, and the email configurations you selected move onto iPhone and are ready for you to use.

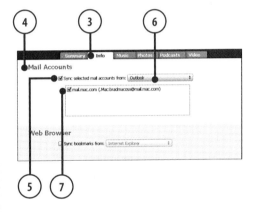

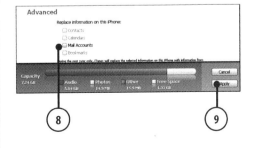

Syncing Email Accounts with a Mac

You can sync email accounts from Mail or Entourage on a Mac with iPhone to quickly configure it to work with email for those accounts.

1. Connect iPhone to your computer.

2. Select iPhone on the Source list in iTunes.

3. Click the Info tab.

4. Scroll down until you see the Mail Accounts section.

5. Check Sync selected Mail accounts from.

6. Check the check box for each account you want to move onto iPhone. You can choose to move any or all of your email to iPhone.

7. If you want the email accounts to replace the accounts currently on iPhone, check Mail Accounts; if you leave this unchecked, the selected email accounts are added to iPhone, leaving those already configured on it unchanged.

8. Click Apply. The sync process runs, and the email configurations you selected move onto iPhone and are ready for you to use.

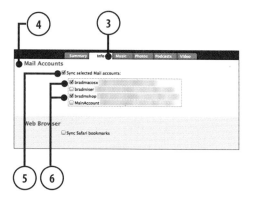

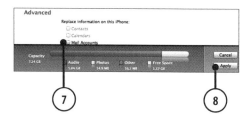

Configuring Email Accounts on iPhone Manually

Configuring email accounts manually on iPhone differs slightly depending on the specific kind of email account you are configuring, but the following example using a GMail account should help you understand how to configure other kinds of accounts.

1. Gather the configuration information for your email account, such as its type, your email address, your username, your password, incoming mail server, and outgoing mail server.

2. On iPhone's Home screen, press Settings. The Settings screen appears.

GMail POPs Is for Me

If you don't have a GMail account, you can sign up for a free one at mail.google.com. When you set up the account, make sure that you select the POP option. If you already have an account, log in to your Google account, choose GMail settings, click the Forwarding and POP tab, choose the Enable POP for all mail option, and save your changes. If your GMail account is not POP-enabled, it won't work on iPhone.

3. Press Mail. The Mail screen appears unless you haven't configured any email accounts on iPhone previously; in that case, the Add Account screen appears, and you can skip step 4.

4. Press Add Account. The Add Account screen appears.

5. Press GMail. If you are configuring email for one of the other services, such as AOL or .Mac, press that service. For an ISP not shown on the list, press Other. The specific details for these other services are slightly different, but the configuration process is very similar to that for GMail. If you select GMail, the GMail screen appears.

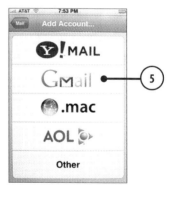

Configuring Other Email Accounts

When you select the Other option, such as to configure an email account from your ISP, the primary difference is that you have to enter more information. When you choose Other, you have to enter all the detail required to access the email account because iPhone doesn't have access to any of it.

6. Enter your name.

7. Enter your GMail address; iPhone adds the "@gmail.com" part for you automatically.

8. Enter your GMail password.

9. Enter a description of the GMail account if you want to; it defaults to your email address.

10. Press Save. The information is checked, and if you entered it correctly, you briefly see a check mark next to each item. If you entered information incorrectly, you see an error message; correct the mistakes and save it again.

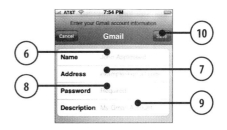

No SSL?

If you see a message about SSL (Secure Sockets Layer, a communication security protocol) not being available when you press Save, just press OK to proceed without SSL. In case you're wondering, SSL is used to encrypt data that is transferred over the Internet. Some email tools can work with SSL connections while others can't. If you can use it, you should, but if you can't, it's not something to worry about.

Configuring Email Accounts for Exchange Servers That Don't Support IMAP

As you read earlier, many Exchange email servers aren't configured to support IMAP access. To use those email accounts on iPhone, you must have additional software or a service. Unfortunately, there isn't room in this book to cover the various options you have. However, an example of one option should help you understand how you can bring these solutions into play on your iPhone.

Many organizations enable email to be available via the Web using Outlook Web Access. You can view email using a website (the URL includes OWA) specific to each organization. After you log in, the resulting window looks and works much like Outlook, but because you can access it via a standard web browser, you don't need to be on your organization's network to access your email. The bad news is that iPhone's Safari application (in its current release) is not compatible with this service. The good news is that some companies provide a service that, in effect, reroutes your Exchange email via the OWA service onto your iPhone so that you can access it there. The other bad news is that you usually have to pay a fee for this service.

In the following example, you learn about a service from a company called Synchronica that reroutes email via an OWA server. At press time, you could try this service for 60 days at no cost. To do this, you must know the URL of the OWA server you use, your email user account (usually everything before the @), and your email password. After you have your OWA information, you can create a Synchronica account and configure iPhone to access it.

>>>*step-by-step*

1. On your computer, open a web browser and move to www.synchronica.com/ syncmldemos/demos.html.

2. Complete the form to register for an account. After Synchronica creates your account, you're prompted to log in to it.

3. Log in to your Synchronica account. You see the Welcome screen.

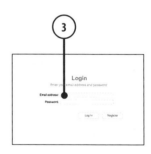

4. Click Setup. You move to the Setup tab.

5. Enter the required information. When you enter your phone number, you have to include the country code, such as +1 for the United States.

6. Click Send.

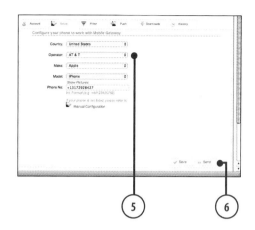

7. Follow the onscreen instructions that lead you through entering your OWA account information. When you finish, you see a screen with a link to manual configuration instructions.

8. Click the Manual configuration instructions link.

9. Click Apple iPhone. The configuration instructions appear.

10. Follow the instructions to complete the configuration of iPhone to access the Mobile Gateway account. Some notes to help you in this follow:

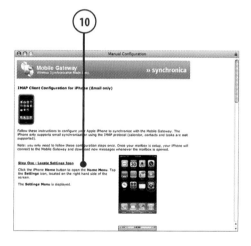

- In step 4, the email address you enter is the email address of your Exchange server account.

- In step 5, you enter the same hostname for both incoming and outgoing servers, which is www.syncml.biz. Don't enter the OWA server information.

- Also in step 5, you enter the password for your mobile gateway account that you created when you registered for it, not your email account's password.

- Step 6 refers to Advanced options, but those don't appear on the current version of mail configuration, so you can skip this step.

11. After you complete the configuration, you can move to the inbox
to start working with the email
or move to the next section to
configure some additional email
settings.

Configuring Global Email Settings

iPhone includes a number of settings that affect all of your email accounts.
You can also set preferences for specific email accounts, as you learn later in
this chapter.

>>>*step-by-step*

1. On iPhone's Home screen, press
Settings. The Settings screen
appears.

2. Press Mail. The Mail screen
appears. In the Accounts section,
you see all the email accounts
configured on iPhone.

3. To have iPhone check your email
automatically, press Auto-Check.
The Auto-Check screen appears.

4. Press the frequency at which you
want iPhone to check for email. It
is marked with a check mark.

5. Press Mail.

6. Press Show. The Show screen appears.

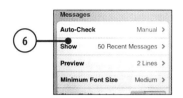

7. Press the number of recent messages you want iPhone to display in the email application.

8. Press Mail.

9. Press Preview. The Preview screen appears.

10. Press the number of lines you want iPhone to display for each email when you view the inbox.

11. Press Mail.

12. Scroll down to see the rest of the settings.

13. Press Minimum Font Size. The Minimum Font Size screen appears.

14. Press the smallest font size you want iPhone to use for email. The larger the size, the easier to read, but the less information fits on a single screen.

15. Press Mail.

16. Press Show To/CC Label to see the To and cc labels in email headers.

17. If you want to have to confirm when you delete messages, turn Ask Before Deleting OFF. Its status becomes ON, and you have to confirm that you want to delete a message when you press its Delete button.

18. If you want to receive a blind copy of each email you send, turn Always Bcc Myself OFF. Each time you send a message, you also receive a copy of it, but your address is not shown to the other recipients.

19. Press Signature. The Signature screen appears.

20. Enter the signature you want to append to each message you send.

21. Press Mail.

22. Press Default Account. The Default Account screen appears.

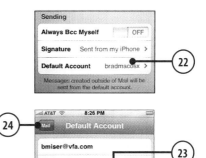

23. Press the account you want to be your default. The default account appears at the top of lists and is used as the From address for emails you send. (You can change it on messages when you send them.) It is also the one used when you send photos, YouTube videos, and so on.

24. Press Mail. You move back to the Mail screen. Now enable or disable email sounds.

25. Press Settings.

26. Press Sounds.

27. To hear a sound when you receive new mail, make sure that the ON status for New Mail is shown; press OFF to turn the new mail sound to ON or press ON to turn it off.

28. To hear a sound when you send mail, make sure that the ON status for Sent Mail is displayed; press ON to turn the sent mail sound off or OFF to turn it on again. Your email configuration is complete.

Working with Email

After you configure email accounts on iPhone, you're ready to start using those accounts for all your email needs. When you move to the Home screen, you see the number of new email messages you have in the Mail button. The Mail button leads you to iPhone's email application.

>>>*step-by-step*

Receiving and Reading Email

1. On the Home screen, press Mail. The Mail application opens, and you move to the last screen you used; if that isn't the Accounts screen, press the return button until you see the Accounts screen. Next to each account, you see the number of new emails received in that account.

Photos Attached

If the message includes a photo, iPhone displays the photo in the body of the email message. You can zoom in or out and scroll to view it just as you can with text.

2. To read messages, press the account whose messages you want to read. iPhone checks for new messages, and you move to that account's screen; the name of the account is the account's description, which defaults to the email address. You see all the folders within that account. The number and type of folders you see depends on the type of email account it is.

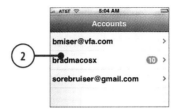

3. Press Inbox. The inbox for that account opens. You see all the messages in the inbox. Unread messages are marked with a blue dot. What you see for each message depends on the settings you made earlier. A paperclip icon indicates that a message includes an attachment. At the bottom of the screen, you see when the inbox was last *updated*, meaning the last time messages were retrieved.

4. Scroll up or down the screen to browse all the messages.

5. To read a message, press it. The message screen appears. As soon as you open a message's screen, it's marked as read, and the email counter reduces by 1. At the top of the screen, you see number of the message and the total in the inbox (such as 2 of 10). Just below that is the address information, including who the message is from and who it was sent to. Under that, you see the message's subject along with time and date it was sent. If the message has an attachment, you see it below the subject line. Last but not least, you see the body of the message.

Attachment

From

Subject

Preview

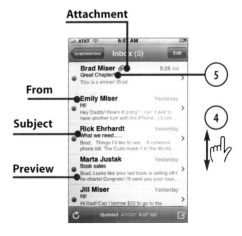

Loading More Messages

If more messages are available than are downloaded, press the Load More Messages link. The additional messages download to the inbox you are viewing.

Address info **Subject, time, and date**

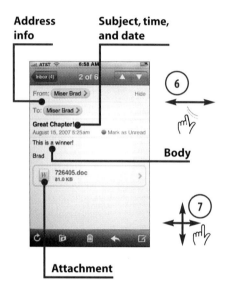

6. Unpinch or double-press your fingers on the message to zoom in. If you double-press on a column of text, it resizes to fit the screen.

7. Drag the message around the screen to read it. To scroll up or down, just drag your finger up or down the screen.

Body

Attachment

8. Pinch your fingers or double-press to zoom out.

9. To view a message's attachment, press it. If iPhone can display files of its type, you see the document on a screen with the document's title as its name.

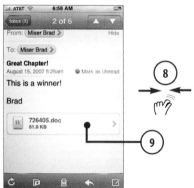

Don't Want to See All the Address Info?

Press the Hide link located just under the down arrow at the top of the email screen to hide address information, such as the To section. Press Details to show that information again; depending on the number of recipients, the iPhone might hide the address information by default. Press Details to see all the information available.

10. Scroll the document by dragging your finger up, down, left, or right on the screen.

11. Unpinch or double-press your fingers to zoom in.

12. Pinch or double-press your fingers to zoom out.

13. Press Message. You move back to the message screen.

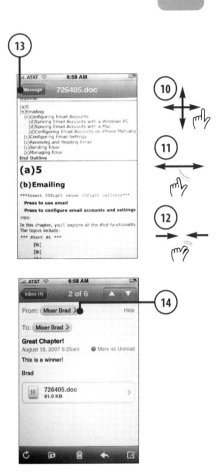

14. To view information for an email address, such as who sent the message, press it. The Info screen appears; its title tells you how the person relates to the message. For example, if you pressed the email address in the From field, the screen title is From. If the person is on your Contacts list, you see his contact information. If not, you see as much information as iPhone can determine based on the email address.

15. Press Message. You move back to the email.

HTML Email

Mail can receive HTML email that behaves like a web page. When you press a link (usually blue text, but can also be photos and other graphics) in such email, Safari opens and takes you to the link's source. You then use Safari to view the web page. See Chapter 6, "Surfing the Web," for information about Safari.

16. To read the next message in the inbox, press the Down arrow. The next message in the Inbox list replaces the current one.

17. To move to a previous message in the inbox, press the Up arrow.

18. To move back to the inbox, press Inbox.

Going Back in Time

If you want a message that you read to be marked as unread again, open it and press Mark as Unread.

Sending Email

You can send email from any of your accounts.

1. Move to the Accounts screen.

2. Press the account from which you want to send email.

3. Press the New Mail button. The New Message screen appears.

4. To type an address to which to
    send the email, press the To field
    and type in the address using
    iPhone's keyboard. As you type,
    iPhone attempts to find a match-
    ing address in your Contacts list
    and displays the matches it finds.
    To select one of them, press it, and
    iPhone enters the rest of the
    address for you.

5. To address the email using
    contacts, press Add Contact. The
    All Contacts screen appears.

6. Use the index and scroll the con-
    tacts to find the contact to which
    you want to send the message.

7. Press the contact to which you
    want to send the message. If the
    contact has more than one email
    address, the Info screen appears. If
    not, the single address is entered,
    you return to the New Message
    screen, and the contact's name is
    shown in the To field; you can skip
    to step 9.

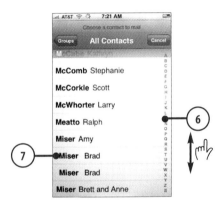

8. Press the email address you want
    to use for the message. You return
    to the New Message screen show-
    ing the contact's name in the To
    field.

Removing Addresses
To remove an address, press it and
then press the Delete button on
iPhone's keyboard.

9. Repeat steps 4 through 8 to add all the recipients to the message.

10. Press in the Cc field.

11. Use steps 4 though 9 to add recipients to the Cc field.

12. Press in the Subject line and type the subject of the message.

13. Press in the body and type the body of the message. iPhone automatically adds your signature; you can leave it as is or change it. As you type, iPhone attempts to correct spelling and makes suggestions to complete words. To accept a proposed change, press the spacebar when the suggestion appears on the screen.

14. When you finish with the message, press Send. iPhone sends the message.

Saving Your Work in Progress

If you want to save a message without sending it, press Cancel. A prompt appears; choose Save to save the message. When you want to work on the message again, move to the account's screen and open the Drafts folder. Press the message, and you move back to the New Message screen as it was when you pressed the Cancel button. You can make more changes to the message and then send it or save it again.

It's Not All Good

You can't add Bcc (blind carbon copy) recipients on email messages. The workaround is to include yourself on the distribution list and then forward the message to anyone you want to receive it, but don't want others to know. You can also forward messages from the Sent folder for your email accounts.

Sending Email from All the Right Places

You can send email from a number of different places on iPhone. For example, you can share a photo with someone by pressing the Email button. Or you can press a contact's email address to send an email from your Contacts list. For yet another example, you can share a YouTube video. In all cases, iPhone creates a new message that includes the appropriate content, such as a photo or link, and you use Mail's tools to complete and send the email.

Replying to Email

Email is all about communication, so Mail makes it simple to reply to messages.

1. Move to the message screen to which you want to reply.

2. Press the Action button. A prompt appears.

3. Press Reply to reply to only the sender or press Reply All to reply to everyone who received the original message. (You only see Reply All if the message was sent to more than one person.) The Re: screen appears showing a new message addressed to just the sender or to everyone who received the message depending on the action you selected. iPhone pastes the contents of the original message at the bottom of the body of the new message, below your signature.

4. Use the message tools to write your reply, to add more To or Cc recipients, or to make any other changes you want.

5. Press Send. iPhone sends your reply.

Forwarding Email

When you receive an email that you think someone else should see, you can forward it to them.

1. Move to the message screen for the message you want to forward.

2. Press the Action button. A prompt appears.

3. Press Forward. The forward screen appears. iPhone pastes the contents of the message you are forwarding at the bottom of the message, below your signature.

4. Address the forwarded message using the same tools that you use when you create a new message.

5. Type your commentary about the message above your signature.

6. Edit the forwarded content as needed.

7. Press Send. iPhone forwards the message.

Large Messages

Some emails, especially HTML messages, are large so that they don't immediately download to iPhone in their entirety. When you forward such messages before they finish downloading, iPhone prompts you to wait until the download finishes before forwarding. If you choose not to wait, iPhone forwards only the downloaded part of the message.

Managing Email

Following are some ways you can manage your email.

Checking for New Messages

Get new mail.

You can check for new mail from any Inbox or message screen by pressing the Get new mail button. iPhone gets and downloads all the email for that account since iPhone last checked it. The bottom of the Inbox screen always shows the status of the most recent check.

Deleting Email from the Message Screen

Delete the message.

To delete a message while viewing it, press the trash can. If you've configured the warning preference, confirm the deletion, and iPhone deletes the message. If you disabled the confirmation, iPhone deletes the message immediately.

Dumpster Diving

As long as an account's trash hasn't been emptied (you learn how to set that later), you can work with a message you've deleted by moving to the account's screen and opening the Trash folder.

>>>*step-by-step*

Deleting Email from the Account Screen

1. Move to the inbox for the account from which you want to delete email.

2. Press Edit. Unlock buttons appear next to each message.

Yet Another Way to Delete

While you are on the Inbox screen, drag your finger to the left or right across a message. The Delete button appears. Press it to delete the message.

3. Press the Unlock button for the message you want to delete. The Delete button appears.

4. Press Delete. iPhone deletes the message.

5. Repeat steps 3 and 4 for other messages you want to delete.

6. Press Done.

Organizing Email

1. Open a message that you want to move to a folder.

2. Press the Mailboxes button. The Mailboxes screen appears. At the top of this screen, you see the current message. Under that, you see the mailboxes available under the current account.

3. Press the folder to which you want to move the message. The message moves to that folder and you move to the next message.

It's Not All Good

You can't create new mail folders on iPhone. To create a new folder for an account, use another tool, such as an email application on your computer or the account's website. New folders become available on the account's screen on iPhone after you sync iPhone.

Managing Email Accounts

You can further configure the way email works by changing each account's advanced settings. You can also get rid of email accounts you don't want on iPhone anymore.

Changing Email Accounts

Each email account has a set of advanced options specific both to the account and to the type of account it is. For example, a .Mac account has one set of options, whereas a GMail account has a different set. The following example shows you how to set advanced options for a .Mac email account. Setting these options for other kinds of accounts is similar.

1. On the Home screen, choose Settings.

2. Press Mail. The Mail screen appears. Each account configured on iPhone is listed.

3. Press the account for which you want to configure the advanced settings. That account's configuration screen appears.

Changing Manual Accounts
If you've configured an email account on iPhone manually, you can use the Edit button on the account's screen to make changes to its configuration. You can't do this for synced accounts because you manage their configuration on your computer.

4. Press Advanced. The Advanced screen appears; the options on this screen depend on the kind of account you are working with. The following steps provide examples of common settings for a .Mac email account.

5. Use the Mailbox Behaviors controls to determine whether the mailboxes used for Drafts, Sent, or Deleted messages are stored on iPhone or only on the mail server. If the messages are stored on the mail server only, your computer must be connected to the Internet to be able to access them. If they are stored on iPhone, you can access them at any time, but they use iPhone memory. To change the location of a mailbox, press it. Its screen appears.

6. To store the folder on your iPhone, press the selection in the On My iPhone section. To store a folder only on the server, press it on the On the Server list. You return to the Advanced screen. iPhone displays On My iPhone next to the mailbox to indicate that it is also stored on iPhone, or it displays the mailbox's name to show that it's stored only on the server.

7. To determine when deleted messages are removed from iPhone, press Remove. You see the Remove screen.

8. Press the amount of time after which you want to remove deleted messages.

9. Press Advanced.

10. If you want incoming mail to use SSL for better security, ensure that the status of Incoming Uses SSL is set to ON.

11. If you want outgoing mail to use SSL, ensure that the status of Outgoing Uses SSL is ON.

12. To change the type of authentication used, press Authentication. The Authentication screen appears.

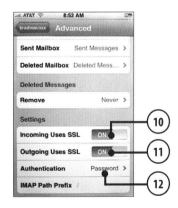

13. Press the type of authentication to use. The provider of the account determines this. The most common type is Password, but other options exist, depending on the kind of account you are using.

14. Press Advanced.

15. If you need to change the path prefix for IMAP accounts, press the IMAP Path Prefix field. The keyboard appears.

16. Enter the path to use.

17. Press the Return button labeled with the account's name.

Deleting Email Accounts

Press if you don't want to receive email from this account on iPhone.

If you no longer want to receive email from an account on iPhone, you can delete it by opening its account screen and pressing Delete Account. If you press Delete Account in the confirmation prompt, iPhone removes the account. Of course, the account still exists; you just won't get email from it on iPhone. You can still use it with an email application, via the Web, and so on. You can restore it to iPhone by syncing it or by re-creating it manually.

It's Not All Good

iPhone's Mail doesn't include any spam tools. If you put an already-spammed address on iPhone, all the spam's going to come right to your iPhone, which can be a nuisance.

The best thing to do is to keep your important addresses from being spammed. Consider using a "sacrificial" email account when you shop, post messages, and in the other places where you're likely to get spammed. If you do get spammed, you can stop using the sacrificial account and create another one to take its place. Or you can delete the sacrificial account from iPhone and continue to use it on your computer where you likely have spam tools in place.

A more complicated way to avoid spam on iPhone is by filtering all email through an account that does have spam filtering. For example, you can create a GMail account and route all your email through it. Use the GMail account's spam tool to manage the spam and then add only that GMail account to iPhone.

Configure
Safari.

Get on
the Web
wherever
you are.

In this chapter, you'll explore all the web browsing functionality that iPhone has to offer. The topics include the following:

→ Configuring Safari settings
→ Moving favorites from a Windows PC to iPhone
→ Moving bookmarks from a Mac to iPhone
→ Browsing the Web

6

Surfing the Web

Wouldn't it be nice to be able to browse the Web wherever you are using a real web browser instead of the modified browsers available on most smart phones? And wouldn't it be nice not to have to be concerned with pages being formatted for proper display on a mobile device? What if you could just use the regular Web on a cell phone? Obviously, since you have an iPhone, you know you have all these niceties because iPhone has a full-featured web browser: Safari.

The Name for the EDGE Doesn't Refer to Its Speed

There are two ways you can connect iPhone to the Internet to surf the Web. One is through the AT&T EDGE network. This method has the benefit of being included with your iPhone plan, and it is widely available. However, it is very, very slow. If you're used to browsing the Web via broadband connections, the performance you get from the EDGE network for the Web will probably be something much less than acceptable. The other way is to use a Wi-Fi connection to get broadband speeds. See Chapter 4, "Connecting to the Internet, Bluetooth Devices, and VPNs," to get iPhone on a Wi-Fi network so that you can reach cruising speed.

Configuring Safari Settings

Before you surf, take a couple of minutes to configure iPhone's Safari settings:

>>>*step-by-step*

1. On the Home screen, press Settings. The Settings screen appears.

2. Scroll down the page until you see Safari.

3. Press Safari. The Safari screen appears.

4. To leave Google as the default search engine, skip to step 7. To change the default search engine from Google to Yahoo!, press Search Engine. The Search Engine screen appears.

5. Press Yahoo!. It is now checked to show you that it is the selected search engine.

6. Press Safari. You move back to the Safari screen, and Yahoo! is shown as the search engine.

7. To disable JavaScript functionality, press JavaScript ON. Its status becomes OFF, to show you it is no longer active. Some web pages might not work properly with JavaScript turned off, but it is more secure. I recommend you leave JavaScript on unless you're sure that the sites you visit don't need it.

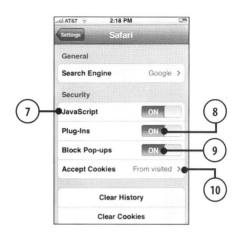

8. To disable plug-ins, press Plug-Ins ON. Its status becomes OFF, and plug-ins no longer work with Safari. Unless you have a very specific reason not to allow plug-ins, leave this enabled so you can get the most functionality possible.

9. To disable pop-up blocking, press Block Pop-ups ON. Its status becomes OFF, and pop-ups are no longer blocked.

10. To configure how cookies are handled, press Accept Cookies. The Accept Cookies screen appears.

11. Press the kind of cookies you want to accept. The None option blocks all cookies. The From visited option accepts cookies only from sites you visit. The Always option accepts all cookies. Most people should choose the From visited option.

12. Press Safari.

13. To clear the history of websites you have visited, press Clear History.

14. Press Clear History at the prompt. This removes the websites you have visited from your history list. The list starts over, so the next site you visit is added to your history list again.

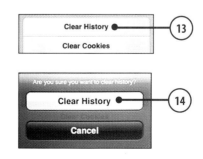

15. To remove all cookies from iPhone, press Clear Cookies.

| Clear History |
| Clear Cookies ● | ── (15)

16. Press Clear Cookies at the prompt. Any sites that require cookies to function re-create the cookies they need the next time you visit them, assuming that you allow cookies.

Are you sure you want to clear all cookies?
| Clear Cookies ● | ── (16)
| **Cancel** |

17. To clear the web browser's cache, scroll down the screen and press Clear Cache.

| Clear History |
| Clear Cookies |
| Clear Cache ● | ── (17)

18. When prompted, press Clear Cache to confirm the action. The next time you visit a site, its content is downloaded to iPhone again. The cache stores information from web sites so that you can return to that information without downloading it from the Web again.

Are you sure you want to clear the cache?
| Clear Cache ● | ── (18)
| **Cancel** |

Moving Favorites from a Windows PC to iPhone

You can move your Internet Explorer favorites or bookmarks from another browser to iPhone so that you can use them to access the same websites on iPhone that you do on your computer.

>>>*step-by-step*

1. Connect iPhone to your computer and open iTunes if it doesn't open automatically.

2. Select iPhone on the Source list.

3. Click the Info tab.

4. Scroll down until you see the Web Browser section.

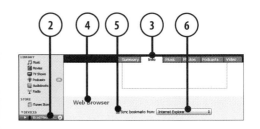

5. Check the Sync bookmarks from check box.

6. Choose the web browser containing the bookmarks or favorites you want to move onto iPhone on the pop-up menu.

7. If you want to replace the bookmarks on iPhone with those you're moving from the PC, check Bookmarks in the Advanced section. If you leave this unchecked, the favorites or bookmarks from the PC are added to those on iPhone.

8. Click Apply. The next time you sync iPhone, your bookmarks or favorites move onto it.

Moving Bookmarks from a Mac to iPhone

You can move your Mac's Safari bookmarks to iPhone so that you can use them to access the same websites on iPhone that you do on your computer.

>>>step-by-step

1. Connect iPhone to your Mac and open iTunes if it doesn't open automatically.

2. Select iPhone on the Source list.

3. Click the Info tab.

4. Scroll down until you see the Web Browser section.

5. Check the Sync Safari bookmarks check box.

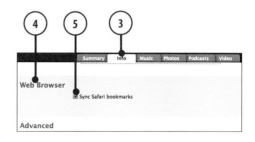

6. If you want the bookmarks you're moving from the Mac to replace those on iPhone, check Bookmarks in the Advanced section. If you leave this unchecked, the bookmarks from the Mac are added to those on iPhone.

7. Click Apply. The next time you sync iPhone, your bookmarks or favorites move onto it.

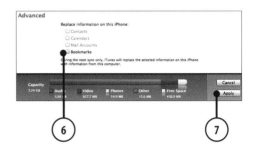

Browsing the Web

If you've used a web browser on a computer before, using Safari on iPhone will be a familiar experience. If you've not used a web browser before, don't worry because using Safari on iPhone is simple and intuitive.

>>>step-by-step

Moving to Websites via Bookmarks

Using bookmarks that you've moved from a computer onto iPhone makes it easy to get to websites that are of interest to you. You can also create bookmarks on iPhone (you learn how later in this section) and use them just like bookmarks you've imported from a computer.

1. On the iPhone Home screen, press Safari. Safari opens.

2. Press the Bookmarks button. The Bookmarks screen appears.

Bookmark folder

3. Scroll up or down the list of bookmarks.

4. To move to a bookmark, skip to step 9. To open a folder of bookmarks, press it. The folder's screen appears.

Bookmark

5. Scroll up or down the folder's screen.

6. Press a folder to move to the bookmarks it contains.

7. To return to a previous screen, press the return button, which is labeled with the name of the last folder you visited or with Bookmarks if the Bookmarks screen was the last one you visited.

8. Repeat steps 5 and 6 until you see a bookmark you want to visit.

9. Press the bookmark you want to visit. Safari moves to that website.

10. Use the information in the section titled "Viewing Websites" to view the web page.

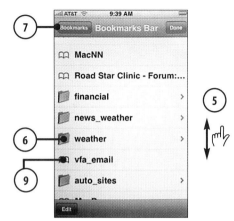

Change Your Mind?

If you decide not to visit a bookmark, press Done. You return to the previous page you were viewing.

Moving to Websites by Typing a URL

Although it might not be fun to type URLs, sometimes that's the only way you have to get to a website.

1. On the iPhone Home screen, press Safari. Safari opens.

2. Press in the Address bar. The keyboard appears along with the
   Search bar. The URL of the
   current web page appears in
   the Address bar.

3. If an address appears in the
   Address bar, press the Clear button to remove it.

4. Type the URL you want to visit. If
   it starts with *www*, you don't have
   to type "www." As you type, Safari
   attempts to match what you are
   typing to a site you have visited
   previously or to one of your bookmarks and presents a list of those
   sites to you.

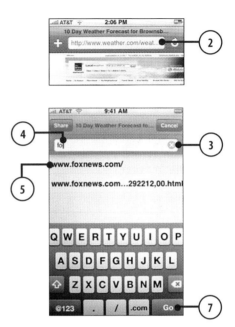

5. If one of the sites shown is the one
   you want to visit, press it. You move
   to that web page; skip to step 8.

6. If Safari doesn't find a match, continue typing until you enter the
   entire URL.

7. Press Go. You move to the web
   page.

8. Use the information in the section
   that follows, titled "Viewing
   Websites," to view the web page.

.com for All
Because so many URLs end in
.com, there's a handy .com key on
the keyboard.

Viewing Websites

Although iPhone has a relatively small screen, it does have a lot of features that make viewing normal-sized web pages possible.

1. Use Safari to move to a web page as described in the previous two sections.

2. To scroll a web page, drag your finger right or left or up or down.

3. To zoom in manually, unpinch your fingers.

4. To zoom in automatically, press your finger on the screen twice.

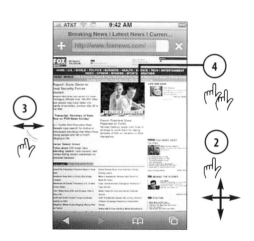

5. To zoom out manually, pinch your fingers.

6. To zoom on a column or a figure, press it twice.

7. To move to a link, press it once. The web page to which the link points opens.

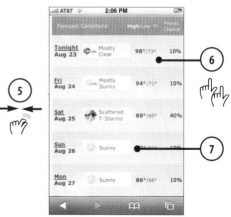

Viewing Links

To zoom a link to see where it points, press your finger on it and hold your finger down. A text balloon pops up to show you the link's information. When you lift your finger, you move to the linked page. If you decide not to visit the link, drag your finger off the link before you lift your finger off the screen.

8. Scroll and zoom on the page to read it.

9. To zoom in or out automatically, press the screen twice.

10. To stop a page while it's loading, press the Stop button.

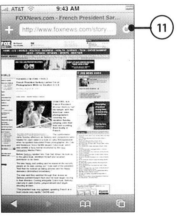

11. To refresh a page, press Refresh.

12. To view the Web in landscape mode, rotate iPhone clockwise.

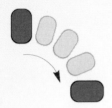

13. To move to a previous page you've visited, press Back.

14. To move to a subsequent page, press Forward.

Where Art Thou, Address Bar?

If you lose sight of the Address bar when you're scrolling pages, press the status bar, where the time displays, once. You scroll to the top of the screen and can see the Address bar again.

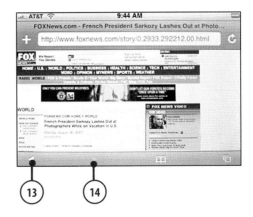

Searching the Web

Earlier you learned that you can use
Safari to search the Web using
Google or Yahoo! Whichever search
engine you choose, you search the
Web the same way.

1. Move to a web page and press
   the Address bar.

2. Press in the Search bar.

3. Type your search word(s). As you
   type, iPhone makes suggestions
   to correct spelling; press the
   spacebar to accept it.

4. Press Google or Yahoo! (the button name depends on the search
   engine you are using). The website performs the search, and you
   see the results on the search
   results page.

5. Use the search results page to
   view the results of your search.
   These pages work just like other
   web pages. You can zoom, scroll,
   and click links to explore results.

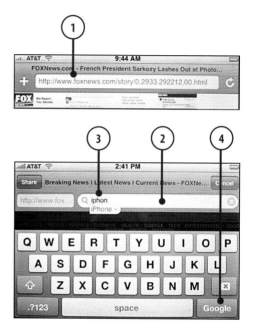

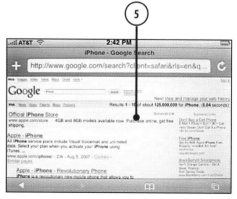

Returning to Previous Websites

As you move about the Web, Safari tracks the sites you visit and builds a history list. You can use this list to return to sites you've visited.

1. Open a web page and press the Bookmarks button. The Bookmarks screen appears.

Safari Has a Good Memory
Safari remembers the last search you did. To clear a search, click the Clear button located at the right end of the Search bar.

2. If necessary, scroll to the top of the page so that you see the History folder.

3. Press History. The History screen appears.

4. Scroll the page to browse all the sites you've visited. The most recent sites appear at the top of the screen. Earlier sites are collected in folders for each day, starting with Earlier Today and moving back one day at a time.

5. To return to a site, skip to step 6. To view sites in one of the folders, press the folder containing the site you want to visit. That date's screen appears.

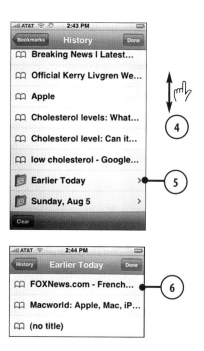

6. Press the site you want to visit. The site opens.

7. Use the techniques you learned earlier in this chapter to view the content of the page.

Saving and Organizing Bookmarks

In addition to moving bookmarks from a computer onto iPhone, you can add new bookmarks on iPhone, and they'll move onto the computer the next time you sync. You can organize bookmarks on iPhone, too.

Saving Bookmarks

1. Move to a web page that you want to save as a bookmark.

2. Press the Add Bookmark button. The Add Bookmark screen appears. The top bar is the name of the bookmark. The second bar shows its URL. The third bar shows where the bookmark will be stored.

3. Edit the bookmark's name as needed.

4. Press Bookmarks. The Bookmarks screen appears. Starting at the top level, Bookmarks, you see all the folders on iPhone in which you can place the new bookmark.

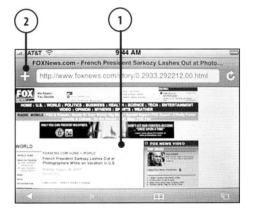

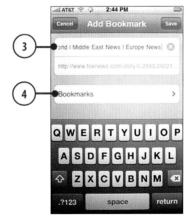

5. Scroll the screen to find the folder in which you want to place the new bookmark. You see folders nested within other folders to show you the hierarchical relationship between them.

6. To choose a location for the new bookmark, press it. You return to the Add Bookmark screen, which shows the location you selected.

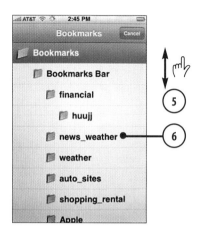

7. Press Save. The bookmark is created and saved in the location you specified. You can use the Bookmarks tool to move to it at any time.

Bookmarks Option?

The location shown in the third bar is the last one in which you stored a bookmark. The first time you add a bookmark, this bar is called Bookmarks because that's the default location. After you choose a different location, the bar is relabeled with that location's name, which iPhone remembers the next time you add a new bookmark.

Organizing Bookmarks

1. Press the Bookmarks button in Safari to move to the Bookmarks screen.

2. Press Edit. The unlock buttons appear next to the folders and bookmarks you can change; some folders, such as the History folder, can't be changed. The order icons also appear.

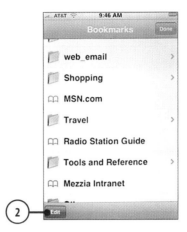

3. Drag the order icon next to bookmarks or folders you want to move up or down the list up or down the screen. As you move between existing items, they slide apart to make room for the folder or bookmark you are dragging. The order of the items on the list is the order they appear.

4. To change the name of a folder or bookmark or the folder in which a bookmark is stored, press it. The Edit Bookmark or Edit Folder screen appears.

5. Change the name in the name bar.

6. If you want to change a bookmark's URL, press the URL bar and make changes to the current URL. When you edit a folder, this bar doesn't appear because it doesn't apply to a folder.

7. To change the location of the folder or bookmark, press the Location bar, which is labeled with the bookmark's current location. The Bookmarks screen appears.

8. Scroll the list of bookmarks until you see the folder in which you want to place the selected bookmark or folder.

9. Press the folder into which you want to move the folder or bookmark you selected. You move back to the Edit Folder or Edit Bookmark screen, and iPhone shows the new location of the bookmark or folder.

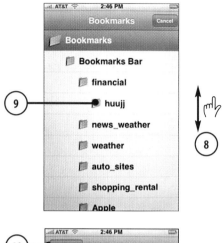

10. Press Bookmarks. You move back to the Bookmarks screen.

11. To create a new folder, press New Folder. The Edit Folder screen appears.

12. Enter the name of the folder.

13. Press Bookmarks. The Bookmarks screen appears.

14. Scroll the list of bookmarks until you see the folder in which you want to place the new folder.

15. Press the folder into which you want to move the new folder. You move back to the Edit Folder screen, which shows the new location of the folder.

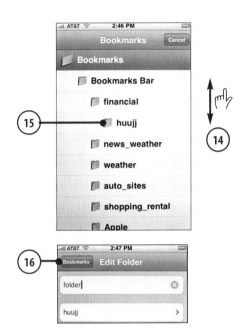

16. Press Bookmarks.

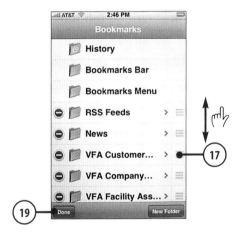

17. Drag the new folder so that it is listed in the order you want it to appear on the Bookmarks screen.

18. Place bookmarks or other folders within the new folder using the techniques you learned earlier to move folders and bookmarks around in existing folders.

19. Press Done. iPhone saves your changes.

Deleting Bookmarks or Folders

1. Press the Bookmarks button in Safari to move to the Bookmarks screen.

2. Press Edit. The unlock buttons appear next to the folders and bookmarks you can change; some folders, such as the History folder, can't be changed. The order icons also appear.

3. Scroll up and down the screen to find the bookmark or folder you want to delete.

4. Press its unlock button. The Delete button appears.

5. Press Delete. The folder or bookmark is deleted. Deleting a folder also deletes all the bookmarks it contains.

6. Repeat steps 4 and 5 to delete other folders or bookmarks.

7. Press Done. You return to the Bookmarks screen.

Completing Web Forms

Just like web browsers on a computer, you can provide information through web pages in Safari by completing forms, such as to log in to your account on a website.

1. Open Safari and move to a website containing a form.

2. Zoom in on the fields you need to complete.

3. Press in a field. The keyboard pops up.

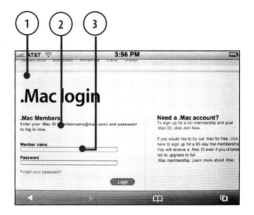

4. Enter the information in the field.

5. Press Next. If there isn't another field on the form, this button is disabled, so skip this step. If it is enabled, you move to the next field on the form.

6. Repeat steps 4 and 5 to complete all the fields on the form.

7. Press Done. The keyboard closes, and you move back to the web page.

8. Press Submit, Go, Login, or another button to provide the form's information to the website.

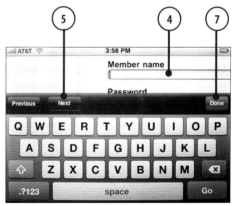

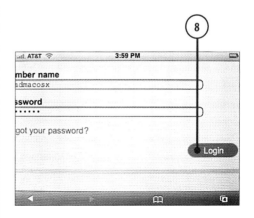

Opening and Managing Multiple Web Pages at the Same Time

Using Safari, you can open and work with multiple web pages at the same time. Some links on web pages open a new page, or you can open a new page manually at any time.

1. Using Safari, open a web page.

2. Press the Page Manager button. The page manager appears.

Safari Keeps Working

As you move to web pages, you can immediately press the Page Manager button to open more pages. Pages continue to load in the background as you move between the Page Manager and individual pages.

3. Press New Page. A new web page opens. The counter on the Page Manager button increases by one to show you how many pages are now open.

4. Use Safari's tools to move to a web page. You can enter a URL, use a bookmark, perform a search, and so on.

5. View and work with the web page.

6. Repeat steps 2 through 5 to open as many web pages as you want to see.

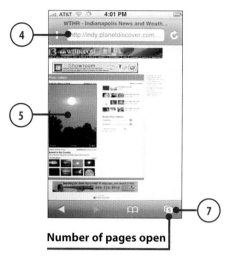

Number of pages open

7. Press the Page Manager button again. You see a thumbnail representation of each open web page.

8. To move between pages, drag your finger to the left or to the right until the page you want view is in focus.

9. To move to the page in focus, press it or press Done. You move to the web page and can view it.

Jump directly to a page by pressing its dot.

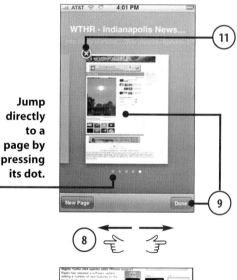

10. Press the Page Manager button. You move back to the Page Manager.

11. To close an open page, press its close button. The page closes and disappears from the Page Manager screen, and the counter is reduced by one.

Communicate while on the move.

Determine if you hear the new text message sound.

In this chapter, you'll explore the text messaging functionality that iPhone has to offer. The topics include the following:

→ Turning the New Text Message sound off or on
→ Sending text messages
→ Receiving and replying to text messages
→ Managing text messages

Text Messaging

Text messaging enables you to have conversations with other people and to communicate information quickly and easily. iPhone has a Text Messaging widget that you can use to send, receive, and converse in text messages. You can maintain any number of conversations with other people at the same time, and iPhone lets you know whenever you receive a new message.

Turning the New Text Message Sound Off or On

When you receive a new text message, iPhone plays an alert tone so that you
know a message has arrived. You can disable this sound if you don't want to
hear it.

>>>*step-by-step*

1. Move the Home screen and
   press Settings. The Settings screen
   appears.

2. Scroll down until you see Sounds.

3. Press Sounds. The Sounds screen
   appears.

4. Press ON next to New Text
   Message. It becomes OFF to show
   you that iPhone won't play the
   alert sound when new text messages arrive.

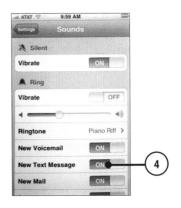

5. To turn the sound back on, press
   OFF next to New Text Message.
   The sound plays, and the status
   becomes ON again.

Sending Text Messages

You can send text messages by entering a number manually or by choosing a
contact from your contacts list.

1. On the Home screen, press
SMS. The Text Messages
screen appears.

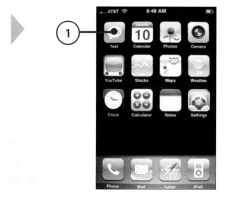

I Didn't Know He Was a Contact

If the number you entered in
step 8 matches a contact on your
contacts list, that person's name
replaces the phone number as
soon as you press the Send bar.

2. Press New Message. The New
Message screen appears.

3. If the person to whom you are
sending the message is not on
your contacts list, skip to step 7.
If the person is on your contacts
list, press Add Contact. The All
Contacts screen appears.

4. Scroll on the screen to find the contact to whom you want to send a message. Remember that you can press a letter on the index to quickly jump to a section of the contacts list.

5. Press the contact to whom you want to send the message. If the person you select has more than one phone number, the contact's Info screen opens. If there is only one number, that number is pasted into the new message, and you return to the New Message screen and can skip step 9.

6. Press the number to which you want to send the text message. You return to the New Message screen; the name of the person you selected is shown in the To field. Skip to step 9.

7. Press the To field.

8. Enter the number to which you want to send the text message. As you type, iPhone tries to match the number you type to someone on your contacts list; it presents a list of numbers and contacts that it thinks matches; press one of these to select it. If the number isn't found, keep entering it until it's complete.

9. Press the Send bar. The keyboard appears.

10. Type the message you want to send.

11. Press Send. The Send status bar appears as the message is sent. When it's complete, you return to the Messages screen if the message was not sent to someone you were previously text messaging with, or you move back to the conversation's screen if you already have a text message conversation going with that person.

Receiving and Replying to Text Messages

When you receive a new text message, you hear the new message tone (unless you've turned it off) and see the new message window on iPhone's screen.

Who message is from

Press to ignore.

Message content

Press to read.

>>>step-by-step

1. Press Ignore if you want to
   ignore the message for now; you
   can always read it later. (See the
   section "Managing Text Messages"
   for details.) Skip the rest of these
   steps.

2. Press View to read the message.
   The message screen appears with
   the person's name as its title. If the
   message is from the same person
   you have already received at least
   one message from or sent one
   message to, the new message
   appears as the last message in the
   conversation toward the bottom
   of the screen. If the message isn't
   part of an existing conversation, it
   appears at the top of a new conversation screen.

3. Read the message.

4. To call the person who sent the
   message to you, press Call. iPhone
   places a call to the number associated with the text message.

5. If the person who sent the
   message is in your contacts list,
   press Contact Info to see her
   information.

6. To reply to the message, press the
   Send bar. The keyboard appears.

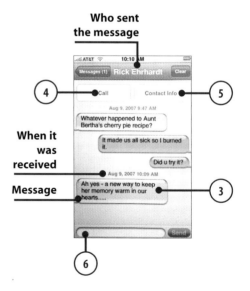

**Who sent
the message**

**When it
was
received**

Message

7. Type your reply.

8. Press Send. The message is sent, and you see your message added to the conversation.

9. If the person replies to you imme- diately, read the reply on the left side of the screen under your message.

10. Repeat steps 6 through 9 to reply and read replies to you.

11. Press Messages. You move to the Text Message screen on which you see all the text message con- versations in progress.

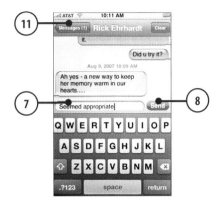

How Many Messages Do I Have?

As you receive new text mes- sages, a red circle on the SMS but- ton on the Home screen indicates the number of new messages you have received. When you read a new message, this number is reduced so that it always indicates how many messages you've received but not read.

Managing Text Messages

As you send and receive messages, the interaction you have with each person becomes a separate text conversation consisting of all the messages that have gone back and forth. You manage these conversations from the Text Messages screen.

Conversing in Text

1. On the Home screen, press SMS. The Text Messages screen appears. On this screen, you see each conversation you have going. The name of the conversation is the name of the person associated with it. If a person can't be associated with it, you see the number you are conversing with. If the message is such that you can't reply to it (for example, when you request information about your AT&T account), you see a number of some sort.

Person with whom you're conversing

When the last message was received

2. Scroll the list to see all the conversations you have on-going.

3. Press a conversation you want to read or reply to. The conversation screen appears; the name of the screen is the person with whom you are conversing, or her number, if she isn't in your contacts list.

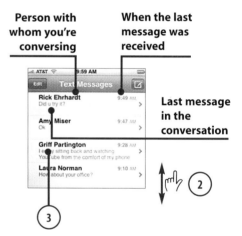

Last message in the conversation

Tired of Typing?
Press Call to call the person with whom you're conversing.

4. Read the messages in the conversation. Your messages are on the right side of the screen in green, whereas the other person's are on the left in gray. Messages are organized so that the newest message is at the bottom of the screen.

5. Scroll the conversation screen to see all the messages it contains.

6. If you don't want to add to the conversation, skip to step 10. To add a new message to the conversation, press in the Send bar. The keyboard appears.

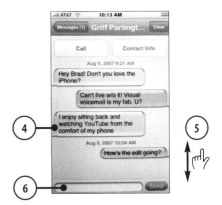

7. Type your message.

8. Press Send. The message is sent, and you see your message added to the conversation.

9. Repeat steps 4 through 8 as long as you want to keep conversing.

10. When you're done, press Messages. You return to the Test Messages screen and see the most recent message in the conversation shown with the date and time it was sent.

Too Many Messages in This Conversation

If you want to get rid of all the messages in a conversation, press Clear, which is located in the top right corner of the conversation screen. This removes all the messages in the conversation, but the conversation remains open so that you can keep it going if you want to.

Press here
to see
where you're
supposed
to be.

Go here to
get all
the time
you need.

Press here
to configure
time and date
settings.

In this chapter, you'll explore all the time functionality that iPhone has to offer. Topics include the following:

→ Configuring iPhone's date, time, and calendar settings
→ Using iPhone as a clock
→ Working with calendars

Working with Date & Time and the Calendar

When it comes to time management, iPhone is definitely your friend. On iPhone, you can have multiple clocks for various locations, and you can have various alarms set on each one. Using iPhone's Calendar widget, you can view calendars that have been synchronized with your computer's calendar using such applications as Outlook on Windows PCs or iCal on Macs; of course, you can also make changes to your calendar on iPhone, and they'll move back to your computer when you sync.

Configuring iPhone's Date, Time, and Calendar Settings

You should configure a few time and date settings before you start using iPhone to manage your time.

>>>*step-by-step*

1. On the Home screen, press Settings.

2. Press General.

3. Press Date & Time. The Date & Time screen appears.

4. To have iPhone display time on a 24-hour clock, press the 24-Hour Time OFF button, which becomes the ON button to show you that iPhone is now showing time on a 24-hr scale. To have iPhone use a 12-hr clock, press ON to turn off 24-hr time.

5. If you don't want iPhone to set its time automatically using the network time it gets from the cell network, press Set Automatically ON. The button becomes OFF, and two additional options appear; follow steps 6 through 21 to set those options or skip to step 22 if you leave the setting for time to be automatically be set by the network, which is the more common option.

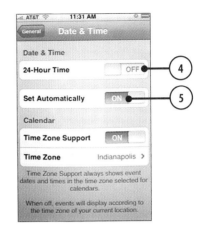

6. Press Time Zone. The Time Zone screen appears.

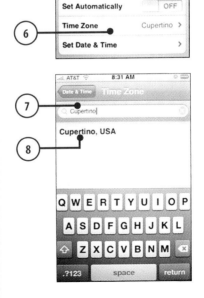

7. Type the name of the city that you want to use to set the time zone. As you type, iPhone lists the cities that match your search.

8. When the city you want to use appears on the list, press it. You move back to the Date & Time screen, which shows the city you selected.

9. Press Set Date & Time. The Date & Time screen appears.

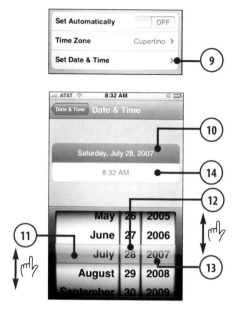

10. Press the date button. The date selection wheel appears.

11. Drag up and down on the month wheel until the center bar shows the month you want to set.

12. Drag up and down the date until the correct day of the month is shown in the center bar.

13. Scroll and select the year in the same way.

14. Press the time button. The time selection wheel appears.

15. Scroll the hour wheel until the center bar shows the hour you want to set.

16. Use the minutes wheel to select the minutes you want to set, as shown in the center bar.

17. Press AM or PM.

18. Press Date & Time. You move back to the Date & Time screen.

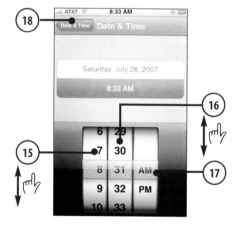

It's Not All Good

The Time Zone Support feature is a bit confusing. If Time Zone Support is on, iPhone displays event times according to the time zone you select rather than your current location. As an example, if you choose Los Angeles, events are always shown based on the time and date in Los Angeles no matter where you are; if you've set a meeting for 10 a.m. in that time zone, it is set for 10 a.m. Los Angeles time regardless of the time zone in which iPhone is located. If Time Zone Support is off, iPhone automatically shifts the times and dates of events to match the time zone of your current location. Your Los Angeles 10 a.m. meeting shows as a 1 p.m. meeting if you are in New York or 12 p.m. if you happen to be in Chicago.

19. To have iPhone display meeting and event times on its calendar based on your current location, press Time Zone Support ON; it becomes OFF to show you that time zone support is disabled. Skip to step 23.

20. If you leave Time Zone Support ON, press Time Zone. The Time Zone screen appears.

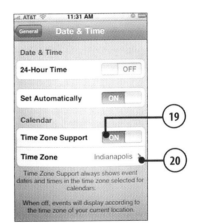

21. Type the name of the city that you want to use to set the time zone. As you type, iPhone lists the cities that match your search.

22. When the city you want to use appears on the list, press it. You move back to the Date & Time screen, and the city you selected is shown.

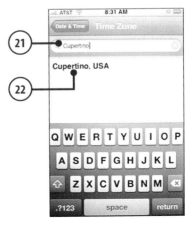

23. Press General. You move back to the General screen and are ready to start using iPhone to manage time and dates.

Using iPhone as a Clock

iPhone is quite a powerful clock. In addition to showing you the time and date where you are currently located (and if you travel a lot as I do, this isn't always obvious), you can set clocks for a variety of locations and set multiple alarms. With iPhone, you might never need a watch or bedside clock again.

Keeping Up with the Time

In the previous section, you learned how to configure iPhone to set its time automatically or allow you to set the time manually. If iPhone sets the time automatically, the current time and date of your location are always shown. If you set the time manually, iPhone continues to display the time and date based on what you set. Unless you have a very specific reason for not wanting iPhone to keep its time and date set to the current cell network, you should leave the time to be set automatically. You can easily configure clocks to show you the current time in specific locations.

Telling Time with iPhone

iPhone displays the current time at the top of many of its screens for easy viewing.

When iPhone is locked and you press the Sleep/Wake button, iPhone shows the current time and date. If you don't unlock iPhone, it goes to sleep again in a few seconds, making this a very easy way to check the current time without using much battery power.

Using the Clock Widget

You can set iPhone to display a number of clocks with each clock having a specific time zone associated with it. This makes it easy to know the time in several locations at once. Even better, you can configure multiple alarms to remind you of important events, such as getting out of bed. The Clock widget also provides a basic but very serviceable stopwatch and timer.

>>>*step-by-step*

Creating, Configuring, and Using Clocks

1. On the Home screen, press Clock. The Clock screen appears.

Like Night and Day

Based on the associated time zone, a clock's face is black if the current time is between sunset and sunrise (in other words, it's dark there) or white if the time there is in daylight hours.

2. Press World Clock. The World Clock screen appears. You see a clock for each location you have configured.

3. To add a clock, press the Add button. The Select City screen appears.

City associated with a clock.   **Time and date in that city**

4. Type the name of the city with which the clock is associated; this determines the clock's time zone. As you type, iPhone tries to match cities to what you are typing and presents a list of matching cities to you.

5. Press the city you want to associate with the clock. You return to the World Clock screen, and the clock is created showing the current time in that city.

6. To remove a clock, press Edit. Unlock buttons appear next to each clock.

Missing City

If iPhone can't find the specific city you want, choose one in the same time zone. The city you select determines the time zone of the clock. However, there is an issue with the clock's name, which is addressed in the "It's Not All Good" section in this task.

7. Press the clock's Unlock button. The Delete button appears.

8. Press Delete. The clock is deleted.

9. Repeat steps 7 and 8 until you've deleted all the clocks you no longer want to see.

10. Press Done.

11. To see all your clocks, scroll up and down the screen by dragging your finger up or down.

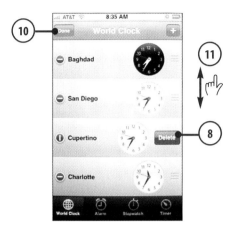

It's Not All Good

Unfortunately, you can't rename clocks to reflect the actual city in which you are interested. So if you can't find the specific city you want when you set the time zone, make sure that you select one that you easily recognize as being in the same time zone as the city where you really want to know the time. You also can't change the order of clocks after they are created; if you want to reorder clocks on the World Clock screen, the easiest way is to just delete all of them and re-create them in the order in which you want them to be shown.

Setting and Using Alarms

1. On the Home screen, press Clock. The Clock screen appears.

2. Press Alarm. The Alarm screen appears. You see the currently set alarms.

3. To add an alarm, press Add. The Add Alarm screen appears.

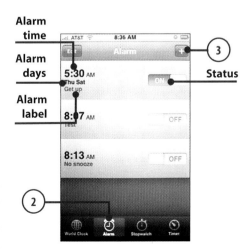

4. To configure the alarm to repeat, press Repeat; to set a one-time alarm, skip to step 8. The Repeat screen appears.

5. Press the day of the week on which you want the alarm to repeat. It is marked with a check mark.

6. Repeat step 5 as many times as you need. The most frequently an alarm can repeat is once each day of the week.

7. Press Back. The Repeat option shows you the days you selected for the alarm to repeat.

8. To choose the alarm sound, press Sound. The Sound screen appears.

Silent Alarm

If you select the None sound, you won't hear anything when the alarm goes off, but a visual alarm displays.

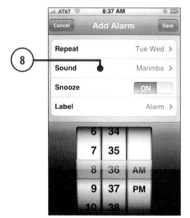

9. Browse the list of available sounds.

10. Press the sound you want to use for the alarm. You hear the sound, and it is marked with a check mark.

11. After you have selected the sound you want to use, press Back. You move back to the Add Alarm screen, which shows the sound you selected.

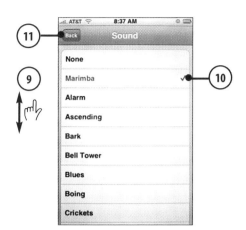

12. To disable the snooze function, press ON. The status becomes OFF. When an alarm sounds and you dismiss it, it won't appear again. With Snooze ON, you can press Snooze to dismiss the alarm, and it returns at 10-minute increments until you dismiss it.

13. To name the alarm, press Label. The Label screen appears with the default label for the alarm. The label is what appears on the screen when the alarm activates, so you usually want to give it a meaningful label.

14. To remove the current label, press the Clear button.

15. Use the keyboard to create a label for the alarm.

16. Press Back. You return to the Add Alarm screen, which shows the label you created.

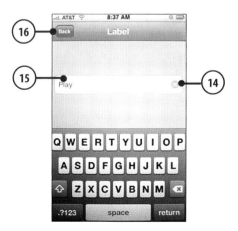

Alarming Volume

The ringer volume setting determines an alarm's volume. As you probably noticed, alarms use the same sounds as the ringer, so this makes sense.

17. Scroll the hour wheel until you see the hour you want to set in the center bar.

18. Scroll the minute wheel until you see the minute you want to set in the center bar.

19. Press AM or PM.

20. Press Save. You return to the Alarm screen, which shows the alarm you set.

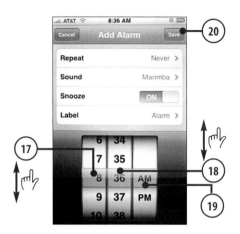

Changing Alarms

You can change existing alarms in several ways.

1. Move to the Alarm screen.

2. Press Edit. Unlock buttons appear next to each alarm.

How iPhone Alarms Are Like Those on Bedside Clocks

You can't set an alarm for a specific date; they are set only by day of the week, just like a bedside alarm clock. To set alarm for a specific date, configure an event on the calendar and associate an alarm with that event.

3. To delete an alarm, press its Unlock button. The Delete button appears.

4. Press Delete. The alarm is deleted.

5. To change an alarm, press it. The Edit Alarm screen appears.

6. Use the controls on the Edit Alarm screen to make changes to the alarm. These work just as they do when you create an alarm. (See the previous steps for details.)

7. Press Save. The alarm is changed, and you return to the Alarms screen.

8. To disable an alarm, press ON. Its status becomes OFF, and it is no longer active.

9. To enable an alarm, press OFF. Its status becomes ON, and it appears at the appropriate times.

Not Dismissed So Easily

When you dismiss an alarm, it isn't deleted, but its status is set to OFF. To re-enable the alarm, move to the Alarm screen and press its OFF button. The status becomes ON, and the alarm activates at the next appropriate time.

Managing Alarms

When at least one alarm is active, you see the Alarm Clock icon in the upper-right corner of the screen next to the Battery icon. When an alarm triggers, you see an onscreen message and hear the sound associated with it. If the alarm is snooze-enabled, press Snooze to dismiss it; it returns in 10 minutes. To dismiss the alarm, press OK.

>>>step-by-step

Using iPhone as a Stopwatch

1. On the Home screen, press Clock. The Clock screen appears.

2. Press Stopwatch. The Stopwatch screen appears.

3. Press Start. The stopwatch starts.

4. To set a lap time, press Lap. The lap time appears on the list below the stopwatch.

5. To stop the time, press Stop. The time stops.

6. To start a new stopwatch session, press Reset. The current time is set to 00:00.0, and all lap times are removed.

Not Seen but Heard

The alarm, stopwatch, or timer continues to work behind the scenes as you move to other screens. So you don't need to be viewing the Timer screen to use the timer, as an example. Set the timer and then keep doing whatever you need to be doing. When something happens you need to know about, iPhone lets you know with onscreen messages or sound.

Using iPhone as a Timer

1. On the Home screen, press Clock. The Clock screen appears.

2. Press Timer. The Timer screen appears.

3. Drag the hour wheel up or down until the center bar shows the hour you want to set on the timer; you can select a timer up to 23 hours.

4. Drag the minute wheel up or down until the center bar shows the minute you want to set on the timer.

5. Press When Timer Ends. The When Timer Ends screen appears.

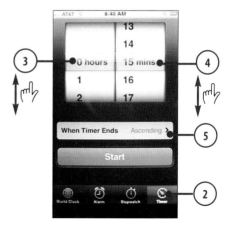

6. Browse the action and sounds available.

7. Press the action or sound you want to associate with the timer. What you select is marked with a check mark. Any sound you select plays.

8. Press Set. You return to the Timer screen, which shows the sound or action you selected.

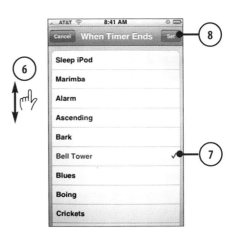

9. Press Start. The countdown begins. When the countdown ends, an onscreen message appears, and the sound you selected plays or iPod functions go to sleep, if you selected that action.

10. To change the sound or action while the timer is counting down, press When Timer Ends and use steps 6 through 8 to choose a different sound or action.

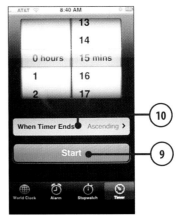

When a timer gets to 0, you see an onscreen message and hear the sound associated with the timer. (If the timer has the Sleep iPod action, you don't hear or see anything, but any music or video playing stops.)

Timer alert

Sleep iPhone Sleep

If you choose the Sleep iPod action, when the timer ends, any iPod functions pause. This is useful when you want music or video to stop playing after a specific time. This works like a sleep timer on a TV.

Working with Calendars

iPhone can help you manage your calendar. In most cases, you'll be moving calendar information from a computer onto iPhone, but you can add events directly to iPhone's calendar. (And when you do, they move to the computer's calendar the next time you sync.)

If you use Outlook on a Windows PC, read the next section. If you use iCal on a Mac, see the section called "Syncing iPhone's Calendar with iCal on Macs." After you sync your calendar, move to the section called "Using iPhone's Calendar."

It's Not All Good

If you don't use Outlook or iCal, you're out of luck on the calendar syncing front. If you don't use one of these calendar applications, but you can access your calendar on the Web, access it using the Safari web browser instead of iPhone's Calendar widget.

>>>*step-by-step*

Syncing iPhone's Calendar with Outlook on Windows PCs

1. Connect iPhone to your computer and open iTunes.

2. Click the Info tab.

3. Scroll until you see the Calendars section.

4. Check Sync calendars from and choose Outlook on the pop-up menu if it isn't selected by default.

5. If you want to prevent older events from being synced, check the Do not sync events older than check box and enter the number of days in the box. Any events older than the number of days you enter are ignored during syncs.

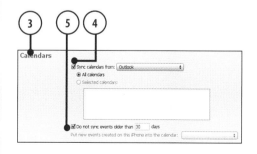

6. Click Apply. The calendar information you selected is moved onto
   iPhone. Each time you sync iPhone
   (if you allow automatic sync, this
   happens every time you connect
   iPhone to your computer), iTunes
   moves changes to your Outlook
   calendar onto iPhone's calendar
   and changes you made on
   iPhone's calendar to your Outlook
   calendar.

Syncing iPhone's Calendar with iCal on Macs

1. Connect iPhone to your computer
   and open iTunes.

2. Click the Info tab.

3. Scroll until you see the Calendars
   section.

4. Check Sync iCal calendars.

5. If you want all the calendars you
   access in iCal to move onto
   iPhone, click the All calendars
   radio button and skip to step 8.

6. If you want only selected calendars
   to move onto iPhone, click the
   Selected calendars radio button.

7. Check the check box next to each
   calendar that you want to sync on
   iPhone.

8. If you want to prevent older
   events from syncing, check the Do
   not sync events older than check
   box and enter the number of days
   in the box.

9. Use the pop up menu to choose
   the iCal calendar on which you
   want to store events that you create on iPhone.

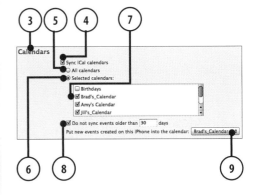

10. Click Apply. The calendar information you selected moves onto
iPhone. Each time you sync
iPhone, iTunes moves the changes
you've made to your iCal calendar
since the last sync onto iPhone's
calendar, and any changes that
you made on iPhone's calendar
move to your iCal calendar.

Using iPhone's Calendar

iPhone's Calendar widget enables
you to view calendar information
and add events to your calendar.

Viewing the Calendar

1. On the Home screen, press
Calendar. The Calendar appears.

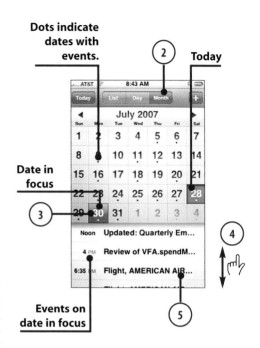

Dots indicate dates with events.

Today

Date in focus

Events on date in focus

2. Press Month. The Month view appears.

3. Press a date in which you are interested. It becomes highlighted in blue, and the event list shows the events associated with that date.

4. Scroll the list of events.

5. To see detailed information for an event, press it. The Event screen appears.

6. Read information about the event; scroll down to see all of it if needed.

7. To change the event, press Edit and follow steps 8 through 10. To delete an event, press Edit and do steps 11 through 13. The Edit screen appears.

8. Use the tools on this screen to make changes to the event. These work just like when you create a new event. (See "Adding Events to the Calendar" for details.)

9. When you finish making changes, press Done. You move back to the Event screen.

10. Press the Return button, now labeled with the current month. You move back to the Calendar window.

11. To remove an event from the calendar, scroll down until you see the Delete Event button.

12. Press Delete Event. The confirmation box appears.

13. Press Delete Event. The event is removed from the calendar, and you return to the Calendar screen.

14. To move ahead to the next month, press Next.

15. To move back to the previous month, press Back.

16. To move the focus to today, press Today.

17. Press List. The view changes to the List view showing each day in a heading with the events for that day immediately underneath the heading.

18. Scroll the list of dates.

19. To view or change an event's details, press it. The Event screen appears; this screen works just as it does when you access it from the Month view. (See steps 8 through 13 for details.)

20. Press Day. The Calendar changes to Day view.

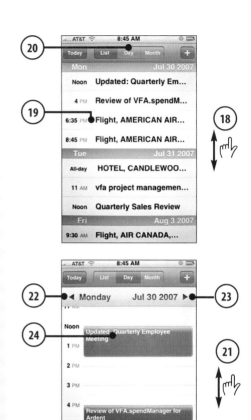

21. Scroll up and down to see the entire day.

22. Press Back to move to the previous day.

23. Press Forward to move to the next day.

24. To view or change an event's details, press it. The Event screen appears; this screen works just as it does when you access it from the Month view. (See steps 8 through 13 for details.)

Adding Events to the Calendar

1. On the Home screen, press Calendar. The Calendar appears.

2. Press Add. The Add Event screen appears.

3. Press Title Location. The Title & Location screen appears.

4. With the cursor in the Title bar, type the title of the event.

5. Press the Location bar and type the location of the event.

6. Press Save. You move back to the Add Event screen.

7. Press Starts Ends. The Start & End screen appears.

8. Press Starts. It is highlighted in blue.

9. Scroll the date wheel until the center bar shows the date of the event.

10. Scroll the hour wheel until the center bar shows the hour of the event.

11. Scroll the minute wheel until the center bar shows the minute of the event.

12. Press AM or PM.

13. Press Ends. It is highlighted in blue.

14. Repeat steps 9-12 to choose the end date.

15. Press Save. You move back to the Add Event screen.

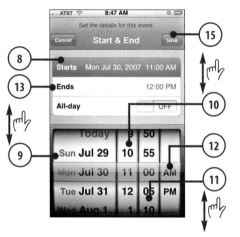

16. To make the event repeat, press Repeat and follow steps 18 through 23. (For a nonrepeating event, skip to step 24.) The Repeat Event screen appears.

17. Press the period on which you want the event repeated, such as Every Day, Every Week, and so on.

18. Press Save. You move back to the Add Event screen.

19. Press End Repeat. The End Repeat screen appears.

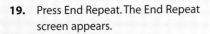

20. To have the event repeat *ad infinitum*, press Repeat Forever.

21. To set an end to the repetition, use the Month, Date, and Year wheels.

22. Press Save. You move back to the Add Event screen.

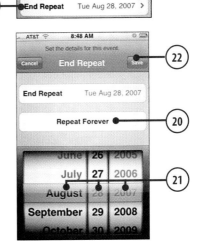

23. To set an alert for the event, press Alert. If you don't want to set an alert, skip to step 30. The Event Alert screen appears.

24. Select when you want to see an alert for the event.

25. Press Save. You move back to the Add Event screen.

Alert, Alert!

To hear a sound when an event alert occurs, open the Sounds screen (choose Home, Settings, General, Sounds), and ensure that ON appears next to Calendar Alerts. If OFF appears, press it to make event alarms audible as well as visual.

26. To set a second alert, press Second Alert. The Event Alert screen appears.

27. Select when you want to see a second alert for the event.

28. Press Save. You move back to the Add Event screen.

29. Press Notes. The Notes screen appears.

30. Type information you want to associate with the event.

31. Press Save. You return to the Add Event screen.

32. Press Done. The event is added to the calendar. Any alarms trigger according to your settings.

Keeping in Sync
When you sync an iPhone, information moves both ways. When you make a change to the calendar from the computer, the changes move to iPhone the next time you sync. Likewise, if you add or change events on iPhone, those changes move to the calendar on the computer during the next sync.

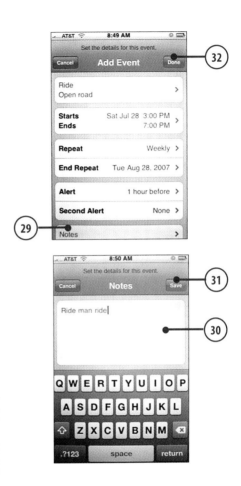

It's Not All Good

Unfortunately, you can't choose the alert sound for an event. All event alarms use the standard calendar event alarm sound.

View photos and slideshows.

Take photos.

Configure slideshow settings.

In this chapter, you'll explore all the photo functionality that iPhone has to offer. Topics include the following:

→ Taking photos with iPhone

→ Moving photos from a computer to iPhone

→ Viewing photos on iPhone

→ Moving photos from iPhone to a computer

Taking, Storing, and Viewing Photos

Although it isn't likely to replace your primary digital camera, iPhone's built-in camera takes reasonable photos, especially given how easy the camera function is to use and the fact that you'll likely have iPhone with you at all times. You can also sync photos between a computer and iPhone.

Whether you've taken them on iPhone or moved them from a computer onto iPhone, you can view your photos individually and as nice slideshows. If you decide some of the photos you've taken on iPhone are worthy of adding to your photo collection, you can move them from iPhone onto your computer.

Taking Photos with iPhone

iPhone's camera lens is located on the backside of iPhone in the upper-left corner. Using iPhone's camera is just about easy as it could be.

>>>*step-by-step*

1. On the Home screen, press Camera. The Camera screen appears; initially it has a shutter, but after a few minutes the window opens, and you start seeing through iPhone's lens.

2. Point the camera at your subject; iPhone is truly point and shoot. (You can't make any adjustments even if you want to.)

3. To capture a photo in landscape mode, rotate iPhone so that it's horizontal.

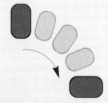

4. When the photo is properly framed, press the Camera button. iPhone snaps the photo, and the shutter closes while the photo is recorded in iPhone's memory. When that's done, the shutter opens again, and you're ready for the next photo.

5. If you want to view the photos you've taken, press the Photos button.

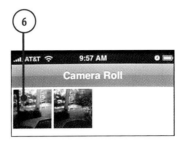

6. Press the photo you want to view. It appears on the screen with iPhone's photo-viewing controls.

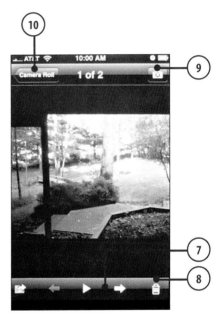

7. Use the photo-viewing tools to view the photo (see "Viewing Photos on iPhone" later in this chapter for the details).

8. To delete a photo, press the Trash can and then press Delete Photo. iPhone deletes the photo, and you see the next photo in the album.

9. If you want to take another photo, press the Camera button.

10. If you want to move back to the photos in the roll, press Camera Roll. You return to the Camera Roll screen.

11. Press the Camera button. iPhone moves back into camera mode.

Syncing Photos

It's a fact that iPhone's memory is somewhat limited, especially if you have a lot of music and video on it. During the sync process, photos take a back seat to other kinds of content, meaning that if there isn't room on iPhone for everything you've selected for a sync, photos are skipped first. It's likely that you won't have enough memory on iPhone for all of your iPhoto photos. Consider creating specific photo albums for the photos you want on iPhone and then choose to sync only those photo albums. You use the memory gauge at the bottom of the iTunes window to get an idea of how much room iPhone has.

12. To take more photos, press the Camera button.

Moving Photos from a Computer to iPhone

iPhone is a great way to take and view your photos while you are on the go. You can move photos from a computer onto iPhone so that you can view them individually and as slideshows. As you might guess, the steps to move photos from a computer to iPhone are slightly different between Windows PCs and Macs. See the section that applies to your computer.

>>>*step-by-step*

Moving Photos from a Windows PC to iPhone

You can use iTunes to move photos you're storing on your PC using Adobe Photoshop Album 2.0 or later or Adobe Photoshop Elements 3.0 or later.

1. Connect iPhone to your computer and open iTunes.

2. Click the Photos tab.

3. Check the Sync photos from check box.

4. On the pop-up menu, choose Photoshop Elements.

5. If you want all the photos in Photoshop Elements to be moved onto iPhone, click the All photos and albums radio button and skip to step 9.

6. If you want only selected albums to be moved onto iPhone, click the Selected albums radio button.

7. Check the check box next to each photo album that you want to sync with iPhone.

8. Change the order in which albums appear by dragging them up and down the list.

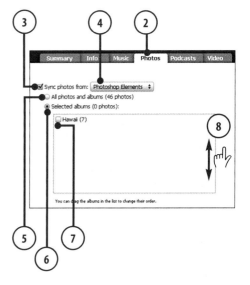

9. Click Apply. The photos you selected move onto iPhone. If you make changes to the photo albums or to the photos you selected, the updates move onto iPhone the next time you sync it.

Moving Photos from a Mac to iPhone

iTunes is designed to work seamlessly with iPhoto. (If you don't use iPhoto, you won't be able to use iTunes to move photos onto iPhone. And if you don't use iPhoto, why not?) You can move all your photos or selected photo albums from iPhoto to iPhone by using iTunes' syncing. You can also move photos you've stored in a folder on your Mac almost as easily.

>>>*step-by-step*

Moving Photos from iPhoto to iPhone

1. Connect iPhone to your computer and open iTunes.

2. Click the Photos tab.

3. Check the Sync photos from check box.

4. On the pop-up menu, choose iPhoto.

5. If you want all the photos in iPhoto to be moved onto iPhone, click the All photos and albums radio button and skip to step 9.

6. If you want only selected albums to move onto iPhone, click the Selected albums radio button.

7. Check the check box next to each photo album that you want to sync on iPhone.

8. Change the order in which albums appear by dragging them up and down the list.

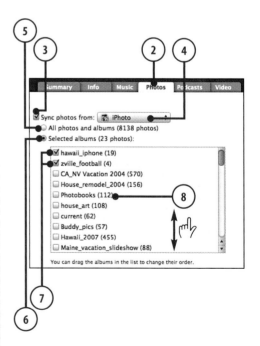

9. Click Apply. The photos you selected move onto iPhone. If you make changes to the photo albums or to the photos in your iPhoto Library (if you can store all of them on iPhone), the updates move onto iPhone the next time you sync it. If there's not enough memory to store the photos you selected, you're warned; you'll need to remove some of the photos from the sync or remove other kinds of content to make more room.

Moving Photos from the Finder to iPhone

1. Connect iPhone to your computer and open iTunes.

2. Click the Photos tab.

3. Check Sync photos from.

4. On the pop-up menu, choose Pictures to import photos from your Home folder's Pictures folder and skip to step 6, or select Choose folder to pick images from a different folder.

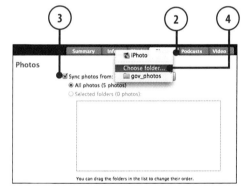

5. If you selected a folder, use the Change Photos Folder Location dialog to move to and select a folder containing the photos you want to move to iPhone. Click Open.

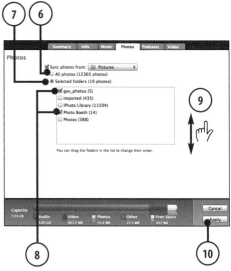

6. If you want all the photos in the selected folder to be moved onto iPhone, click the All photos radio button and skip to step 10.

7. If you want only photos from selected folders to move onto iPhone, click the Selected folders radio button.

8. Check the check box next to each folder that you want to sync on iPhone.

9. Change the order in which folders appear by dragging them up and down the list.

10. Click Apply. The photos you selected move onto iPhone. If there's not enough memory to store the photos you selected, you're warned; you'll need to remove some of the photos from the sync or remove other kinds of content to make more room on iPhone.

Viewing Photos on iPhone

After you've loaded iPhone with great (and maybe a few not-so-great) photos, you can use the Photos widget to view them individually and as slideshows.

>>>*step-by-step*

Viewing Photos Individually

Any photo on iPhone, whether you've taken it with iPhone's camera or moved it onto iPhone via a sync, can be viewed at any time.

1. On the Home screen, press Photos. The Photo Albums screen appears.

2. Browse the screen until you see an album containing photos you want to view.

3. Press the album you want to view. You see the preview screen for that album with a thumbnail for each photo it contains.

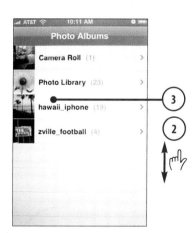

4. To view a photo, press it. The photo display screen appears. When the photo first appears, the photo viewing controls appear on the screen. After a moment, they disappear.

5. To view the photo in landscape orientation, rotate iPhone.

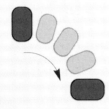

6. Unpinch or double-press on the photo to zoom in.

7. Pinch or double-press on the photo to zoom out.

8. Drag on the photo to scroll in it.

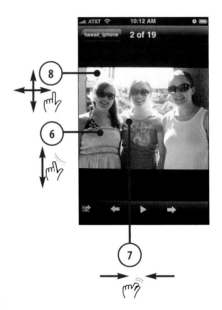

9. Press once to view the controls to see them after they disappear.

10. Press Back or drag quickly to the left to view the previous photo in the album.

11. Press Forward or drag quickly to the right to view the next photo in the album.

12. Press Play to start a slideshow (more on this in the next section).

13. Press the Action button. The action buttons appear. Set the photo as wallpaper using steps 14 through 16. Email a photo using steps 17 through 18. Assign a photo to a contact using steps 19 through 23.

14. To use the photo as wallpaper, press Use As Wallpaper. The Move and Scale screen appears.

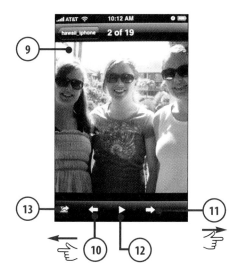

Deleting Contact Photos

When a photo is associated with a contact, even if you delete the original photo taken with iPhone, the photo remains with the contact. (You can only delete photos taken with iPhone; photos that are transferred from a computer must be removed from the sync to be removed from iPhone.) Contact photos are quite small, so don't worry about using lots of iPhone's memory.

15. Drag and pinch or unpinch the image until the part you want to use as wallpaper shows on the screen the way you want to see it as wallpaper.

16. Press Set Wallpaper. The wallpaper is set, and you return to the photo.

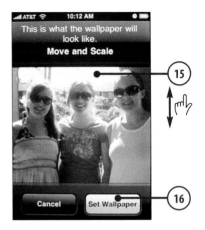

17. To email the photo, press Email Photo. A new email message is created, and the photo is included as an attachment.

18. Use the email tools to address the email, add a subject, type the body, and send it. (See Chapter 5, "Emailing," for detailed informa-tion about using iPhone email.) After you send the email, you move back to the photo.

19. To associate a photo with a con-tact, press Assign To Contact. The All Contacts screen appears.

20. Browse for the contact to which you want to add the photo.

21. Press the contact with which you want to associate the photo. The Move and Scale screen appears.

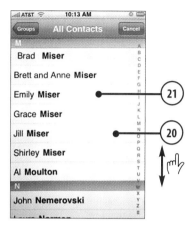

22. Drag and pinch or unpinch the image until the part you want to add to the contact shows on the screen the way you want to see it for the contact.

23. Press Set Photo. The photo is saved to the contact; when iPhone interacts with that contact, such as when you receive a call, the photo is displayed on iPhone's screen. You return to the photo.

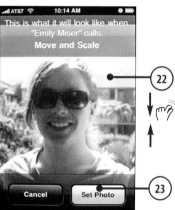

24. When you finish viewing the photo, press the return button, which is labeled with the name of the album. You move back to the album's preview screen.

25. Press Photo Albums. You move back to the Photo Albums screen.

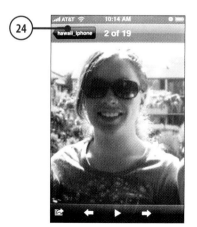

Viewing Photos as a Slideshow

You can view photos as slideshows so that they play with settings and properties you configure.

>>>*step-by-step*

Configure Slideshow Settings

1. On the Home screen, press Settings. The Settings screen appears.

2. Scroll down until you see Photos.

3. Press Photos. The Photos setting screen appears.

4. Press Play Each Slide For.

5. Press the amount of time you want each slide in a slideshow to appear on the screen.

6. Press Photos.

7. Press Transition.

8. Press the transition you want to use when slides change.

9. Press Photos.

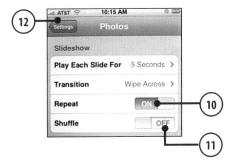

10. To make slideshows repeat until you stop them, press Repeat OFF. Its status becomes ON to indicate that you have to stop slideshows manually. When the status is OFF, slideshows play through once and then stop.

11. To view photos in a random order in a slideshow, press Shuffle OFF. Its status becomes ON so that you know photos appear in random order. To have photos appear in the order they are in the select album, press ON so that the status becomes OFF.

12. Press Settings.

Watching Slideshows

1. On the Home screen, press Photos. The Photo Albums screen appears.

2. Browse the screen until you see an album containing photos you want to view in a slideshow.

3. Press the album you want to view in a slideshow. The album's pre-view screen appears.

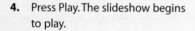

4. Press Play. The slideshow begins to play.

It's Not All Good

Unfortunately, you can't associate music with a slideshow so that the music plays automatically when you watch the slideshow. If you want to hear music while a slideshow plays, use the iPod functions to start the music and then move to and start the slideshow.

5. To view the slideshow in land-scape mode, rotate iPhone in the clockwise direction. The slideshow plays; each slide appears on the screen for the length of time you set. The transition you selected is used to move between photos. If you set slideshows to repeat, the slideshow plays until you stop it; if not, it stops after each photo has been shown once.

6. To pause the slideshow, press the screen. The photo controls appear, and the slideshow pauses at the current photo.

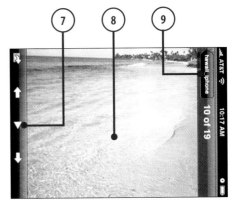

7. Press Play to start the slideshow again. When the slideshow finish-es, you return to the album's pre-view screen.

8. To stop a slideshow, press the screen. The controls appear.

9. Press the return button, which is labeled with the album's name. You move back to the album's preview screen.

10. Press Photo Albums. You move back to the Photo Albums screen.

Moving Photos from iPhone to a Computer

As you use iPhone for a camera, you're going to want to move some of the photos you capture to your computer. How you do this depends on the photo application you use.

>>>*step-by-step*

Moving Photos from iPhone to a Windows PC

How you move photos from iPhone to a Windows PC depends on the specific application you use to manage your digital photos. Most applications designed to import photos from a digital camera should also work with iPhone. One example is Adobe Photoshop Elements.

1. Connect iPhone to the computer. If new photos are detected, the Apple iPhone dialog appears.

2. Select Photoshop Elements.

3. Check the Always use this program for this action check box.

4. Click OK. The Photoshop Elements Photo Downloader appears.

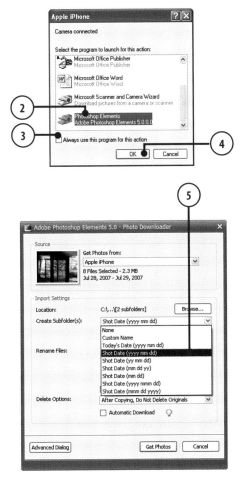

5. To create subfolders for each photo session on iPhone, open the Create Subfolders menu and choose how you want to name the subfolders.

6. If you want to rename the files, use the Rename Files menu.

7. Check the Open Organizer when Finished check box.

8. Use the Delete Options menu to determine what happens to the photos on iPhone after they are imported. The best option is After Copying, Verify and Delete Originals because it frees up space on iPhone while ensuring the photos have been imported successfully.

9. Click Get Photos. Photos move from iPhone into Photoshop Elements, and the application opens.

10. Use Photoshop Elements to work with the photos you imported.

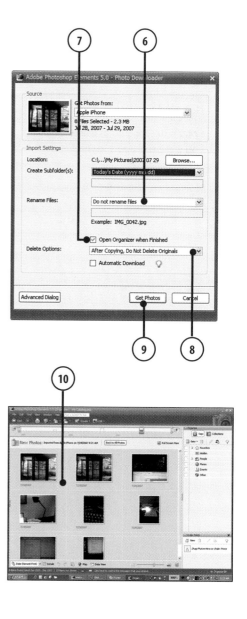

Moving Photos from iPhone to a Mac

iPhone is designed to move its photos into your iPhoto Library easily.

1. Connect iPhone to a Mac. iPhoto opens automatically and moves into Import mode.

2. Enter a roll name for the photos you want to import in the Roll Name field.

3. Enter a description of the photos you want to import in the Description field.

4. If you want photos you import to be deleted from iPhone after you import them, check the Delete items from camera after importing check box.

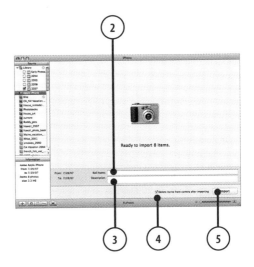

5. Click Import. If you selected the delete option, a warning dialog appears.

6. Click Delete Originals if you want to delete them or Keep Originals if you change your mind and want to leave them on iPhone. The photos move from iPhone into iPhoto.

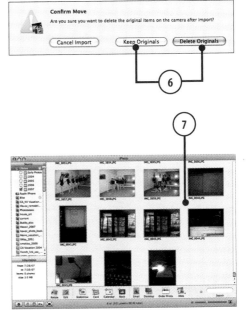

7. Use iPhoto to work with the photos you imported from iPhone.

Cool iPhone
widgets

In this chapter, you'll explore some of the smaller, but still useful and fun, iPhone widgets. The topics include the following:

- → Watching YouTube video
- → Watching stocks
- → Finding your way with iPhone maps
- → Watching the weather
- → Using the Calculator
- → Working with notes

Using Other iPhone Widgets

If you've read through this book to this point, you've already learned enough great iPhone tricks that you're probably convinced iPhone is one of the most useful, not to mention one of the coolest, gadgets ever. Here's where you get some icing on that nice iPhone cake.

Fast Internet for Best Results

Most of the widgets covered in this chapter get information from the Internet. For the best performance, you should connect the iPhone to the Internet via Wi-Fi. If you don't have access to Wi-Fi and use the AT&T EDGE network, some of these widgets are so slow they are basically unusable, which is too bad. For example, being able to use the Map widget wherever you are would be handy, but on the EDGE network, this widget is so slow that you'll need the patience of Job to use it. However, if you can connect via Wi-Fi, you might wonder how you ever got along without some of these goodies. To learn how to connect to the Internet via Wi-Fi and the EDGE network, see Chapter 4, "Connecting to the Internet, Bluetooth Devices, and VPNs."

Watching YouTube Video

You've probably received a link or two to YouTube videos, or you might have watched them via a web browser, such as Internet Explorer or Safari. The beauty of YouTube videos is definitely in the eye of the beholder, but some of them are quite hilarious, and many are shocking or just downright obscene. But if you want to see a video of something, it's probably on YouTube.

Finding YouTube Videos

In this section, you'll learn about some of the more useful ways to find YouTube videos that you might want to watch.

>>>*step-by-step*

Searching for YouTube Videos

1. Move to the iPhone Home screen and press YouTube. The YouTube Home page appears.

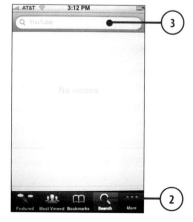

2. Press Search.

3. Press in the Search bar at the top of the screen. The iPhone keyboard appears.

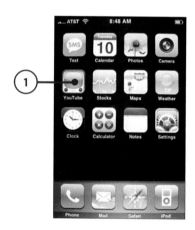

iPhone's search suggestion

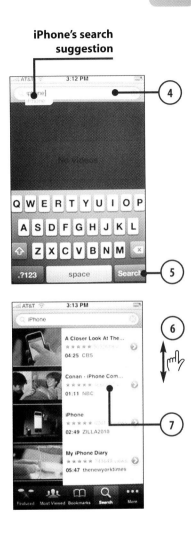

4. Enter the topic for which you want to search. As you type, iPhone tries to complete the term for you. If it presents a term you want to use, press the spacebar on iPhone's keypad.

5. Press Search. The widget searches for YouTube videos that meet your topic search and presents them to you on the results screen. You see a thumbnail view along with the clip's name, rating, number of views, length, and source.

6. Drag your finger up and down the screen to browse the videos in the found set. When you browse to the bottom of the list, press Load 25 More to load more videos.

7. When you find a video you want to view, press it.

8. Rotate iPhone to view videos in landscape mode. The video loads and starts to play.

9. Use the YouTube video controls to control the video. (See the "Viewing YouTube Videos" task later in this section for details.) When the video finishes, the video's screen appears.

10. Use the video's screen to read more information, share it, and so on. (See the "Viewing YouTube Videos" task later in this section for details.)

11. To return to the list of videos found during your search, press Search.

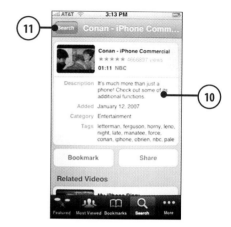

Browsing Featured YouTube Videos

1. Move to the iPhone Home screen and press YouTube. The YouTube Home page appears.

2. Press Featured.

3. Drag your finger up and down the screen to browse the videos in the featured category.

4. When you browse to the bottom of the list, press Load 25 More to load more videos.

5. When you find a video you want to view, press it.

6. Rotate iPhone to view videos in landscape mode. The video loads and starts to play.

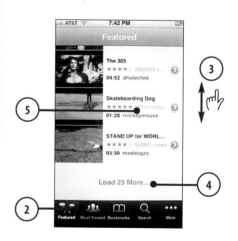

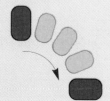

7. Use the YouTube video controls to control the video. (See the "Viewing YouTube Videos" task later in this section for details.) When the video finishes, the video's screen appears.

8. Use the video's screen to read more information, share it, and so on.

9. To return to the list of featured videos, press Featured.

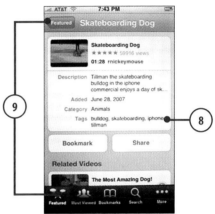

Browsing Most Viewed YouTube Videos

1. Move to the iPhone Home screen and press YouTube. The YouTube Home page appears.

2. Press Most Viewed.

3. To see the videos that have been viewed the most, press All; to see those viewed most today, press Today; to see those viewed most this week, press This Week. The videos that match your criterion are shown.

4. Drag your finger up and down the screen to browse the videos. When you browse to the bottom of the list, press Load 25 More to load more videos.

5. When you find a video you want to view, press it.

6. Rotate iPhone to view videos in landscape mode. The video loads and starts to play.

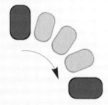

7. Use the YouTube video controls to control the video. (See the "Viewing YouTube Videos" task later in this section for details.) When the video finishes, the video's screen appears.

8. Use the video's screen to read more information, share it, and so on. (See the "Viewing YouTube Videos" task later in this section for details.)

9. To return to the list of most viewed videos, press Most Viewed.

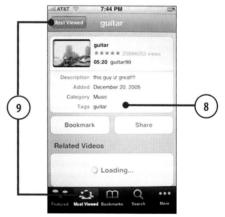

Bookmarking YouTube Videos

As you watch YouTube videos, you can bookmark them so that you can easily watch them again later.

**Press to
bookmark
a video.**

When you finish watching a video and want to bookmark it, press Bookmark. The button grays out to indicate that the video has been added to your YouTube bookmarks.

Bookmark While You Watch
You can also bookmark a video while watching it by bringing up the video controls and pressing the Bookmark button, which is the open book icon on the left end of the video toolbar.

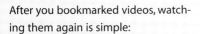
>>>step-by-step

Viewing Bookmarked
YouTube Videos

After you bookmarked videos, watching them again is simple:

1. Move to iPhone Home screen and
    press YouTube.

2. Press Bookmarks. The list of videos that you've bookmarked appears.

3. Drag your finger up and down the screen to browse the videos.

4. When you find a video you want to watch, press it.

5. Rotate iPhone to view videos in landscape mode.

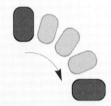

The video loads and starts to play.

6. Use the YouTube video controls to control the video. (See the "Viewing YouTube Videos" task later in this section for details.)

When the video finishes, the video's screen appears.

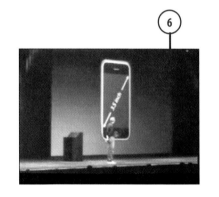

7. Use the video's screen to read more information, share it, and so on. (See the "Viewing YouTube Videos" task later in this section for details.)

8. To return to your bookmarks, press Bookmarks.

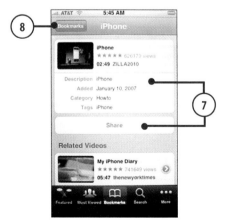

Deleting YouTube Bookmarks

You can also remove your YouTube
bookmarks when you no longer want
them:

1. Move to the Bookmarks page of
   the YouTube screen.

2. Press Edit. Unlock buttons appear
   next to each video.

3. Press the Unlock button for the
   video you want to delete. The
   Delete button appears.

4. Press Delete. The bookmark is
   deleted from iPhone.

5. Repeat steps 3 and 4 to delete
   other bookmarks.

6. When you're done deleting bookmarks, press Done.

Where Art Thou Bookmark Button?

If you've already bookmarked a
video, the Bookmark button
doesn't appear on its screen.

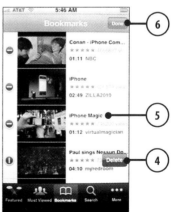

Using the More Menu to Find YouTube Videos

The categories on the YouTube tool-bar are not the only way to find videos. You can use the aptly named More menu to access additional categories.

1. Move to the YouTube screen.

2. Press More. You see the More menu. The additional categories on this menu include Most Recent, which contains videos most recently uploaded to YouTube; Top Rated, which contains videos that have been rated the highest by viewers; and History, which contains videos that you've viewed.

3. Press the category of video in which you are interested. The videos in that category are shown.

4. Browse and watch videos in the selected category just as you watched those described in previous tasks.

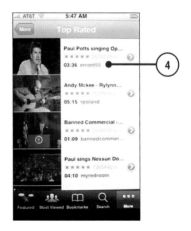

Erase My Past

To clear your video history, move to the History category and press Clear. Press Clear History at the prompt, and the history list for YouTube videos clears. It starts to build again as soon as you watch more videos.

Viewing YouTube Videos

No matter how you find YouTube videos, you use the same controls to watch and work with those videos:

1. Press the video you want to view.

2. Rotate iPhone as the video begins to play.

3. Press the video. The video controls appear.

4. Drag the playhead to the right to move ahead in the video or to the left to move back in the video.

5. Press Scale to scale the video to fill the screen or to restore the video to its original proportions.

6. Press the Bookmark button to bookmark the video.

7. Drag the slider to the left to decrease volume or to the right to increase it.

8. Press Rewind to move to the start of the video or press and hold Rewind to rewind it.

9. Press Pause to pause the video or Play to start it again.

10. Press and hold Fast Forward to fast forward the video.

11. Press Share to share the video. (The detailed steps are in the next section.)

12. To stop the video before it finishes, press Done.

Elapsed time   ④   **Remaining time**   ⑤

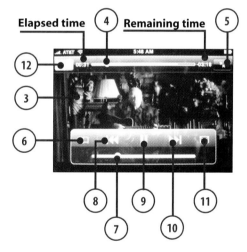

13. Read more information about the video.

14. Press Bookmark to bookmark the video.

15. Press Share to share the video. (The detailed steps are in the next section.)

16. Scroll down the screen to see videos related to the one you watched; watch one of these videos by pressing it.

17. Press the return button to return to the screen from which you selected the video.

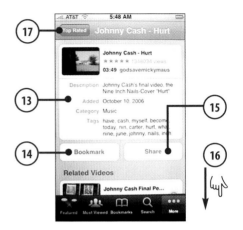

Sharing YouTube Videos

One of the neat things about YouTube videos is that they are designed to be shared; iPhone makes sharing YouTube videos easy.

1. While watching a video, press the Share button. Or from the video's screen, press Share. An email is created with a link to the video and a subject. The iPhone keyboard also appears.

Ditch Someone

To remove a person from the To or Cc list, press the person's name and press the Delete key.

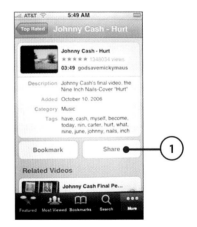

2. Enter the address of the person with whom you want to share the video.

3. Press return.

4. To choose an address from your contacts, press Choose Contact. The All Contacts screen appears.

5. Scroll the screen to find the person with whom you want to share the video.

6. Press the person's name. You return to the email form, and the contact you selected is added to the To list.

7. Continue adding names to the To list until you've added all of them.

8. Use the Cc field to copy people on the email.

9. Press the Subject line and edit the subject line as needed.

10. Press in the body and edit the body text as needed.

11. Press Send. The email is sent, and the recipients are able to use its link to view the video you shared.

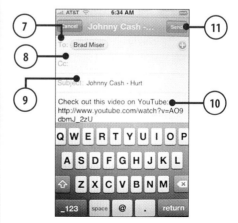

Easy Addressing

As you type an address, iPhone tries to match what you type with an entry in your contacts or with an address you previously sent email to or from which you've received it. If iPhone finds the address you want to use, press it to enter it in the To field.

Recipients click this link to view the YouTube video you shared.

Customizing the YouTube Toolbar

The YouTube toolbar makes it easy to get to specific categories of videos you might want to view. Earlier in this chapter, you learned how to use some of the buttons on this toolbar. You can customize the toolbar so that it contains the categories you use most often.

1. Move to the YouTube screen.

2. Press More.

3. Press Edit. The Configure screen appears.

4. Drag the buttons you want to place on the toolbar from the upper part of the screen onto the location on the toolbar where you want them to appear.

5. Continue placing buttons on the toolbar until you have placed the four you use most frequently there. When you have the toolbar the way you want it, press the Done button.

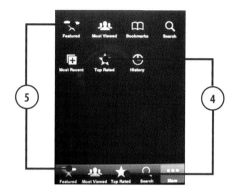

Watching Stocks

iPhone's Stock widget can help you monitor stocks in which you are interested. First, set up the stocks you want to track. Second, track those stocks.

>>>step-by-step

Configuring the Stock Widget

You can add any stock to the Stock widget; all you need to know is the stock's ticker symbol, which you can easily find on the Web.

1. Move to the iPhone Home screen and press Stocks. The Stocks widget appears. You see the stocks currently configured for the widget. At the bottom of the screen, you see the current status of the stock markets.

2. Press the Info button. The Stocks screen appears; on this screen, you configure the stocks you want to track.

Stocks being tracked

3. To remove a stock from the list, press its Unlock button. The Delete key appears.

4. Press Delete. The stock is removed from the widget.

5. To add a stock, press the Add button. The Add Stock screen appears.

6. Enter the stock's symbol or as much as you know of it.

7. Press Search. The widget searches for stock symbols based on what you entered.

8. Scroll the list of stocks.

9. Press a stock you want to add to the widget. You return to the Stocks screen, and the stock you pressed is added to the list.

   Repeat steps 3 through 9 to remove or add stocks until the Stocks screen shows the stocks you want to track.

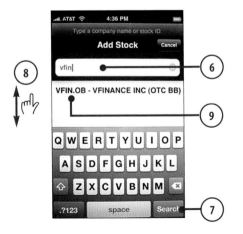

10. Press the Percent button if you want changes to stock values to display as a percentage.

11. Press Numbers if you want changes to stock values to display as a dollar amount.

12. Press Done. You return to the Stocks widget and see the stocks you have configured in the upper part of the screen.

It's Not All Good

Unfortunately, you can't move the stocks up and down the list. They appear in the order in which you added them to the list. To get the stocks in a specific order, you have to add them in that order. So if you want a stock to be at the top of the screen, you have to delete the stocks above it until the one you want at the top is at the top. Of course, you can easily re-add stocks, so this isn't a huge deal. But it is annoying if you want to see the list in a specific order.

>>>step-by-step

Tracking Stocks

With the Stocks widget customized to your stock interests, you can quickly see how your favorite stocks are performing:

1. Move to the iPhone Home screen and press Stocks. The list of stocks you configured appears.

Current value

Stock symbol

Change (% or $)

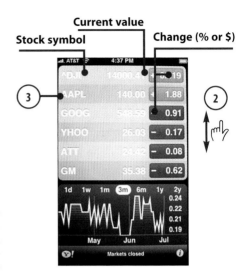

2. Scroll up or down the screen to see the entire list of stocks.

3. Press the stock in which you are interested. The value graph at the bottom of the screen is updated to show the stock you selected.

Getting Back to Stocks

After you're done with the Yahoo! page, press the Home button and then the Stock button to return to the Stocks widget.

4. Press the timeframe in which you're interested, from 1 day to 2 years. The graph refreshes to cover the period you selected.

5. Press the Yahoo! button. The web browser opens and moves to a Yahoo! page for the stock.

6. Use the page to read about the stock.

Dollars or Percent: You Make the Call

To switch between the percentage change and dollar change views, press the Change button for one of the stocks. The changes for all stocks will switch to the other view.

Finding Your Way with iPhone Maps

The Maps widget just might be the coolest one, at least if you are direction-ally challenged like I am. Using the Maps widget, you can find the location of addresses using Google Maps. You can also get directions from one address to another. The maps are linked to your contacts, so you can quickly show the location of any address in your contacts on a map and then get driving direc-tions. You can even see current traffic conditions along the way.

A number of ways exist to find locations on the map. After you find a loca-tion, there are a number of ways to use the information you find, such as to create directions.

To open the Maps widget, press the Maps button on the iPhone Home page. The widget appears, and you can start finding your way.

>>>*step-by-step*

Finding a Location by Searching

You can search for locations in many ways. Your search can be very specif-ic, such as an address, or your search can be more general, such as a search for gas stations or restaurants.

1. Press in the Search box. The key-board appears.

Easy Searching
As you enter a search, iPhone attempts to match what you type with recent searches. As it finds matches, it presents the list of matches to you. Click a search on the list to perform it.

2. Type your search. You can enter an address, city, category, or just about anything else. The more specific your search, the more likely it is that you'll find the location. But general searches can be helpful, such as a search for gas stations.

3. Press Search. The map appears, and the locations that meet your search criteria are marked with a push pin.

4. To see information about a location, press its push pin. The location's menu appears.

5. Use the information in the "Working with Maps" task to find out more information about the location and to change the map's view.

Clear a Search

To clear a search, press the Clear button, which is the gray circle containing an "x," located at the right end of the Search bar.

Finding a Location via Contacts

You can quickly jump to a map of any address in your contact list.

1. Press the Lists button. The Lists tool appears.

One Address Only

If a contact has only one address, when you press it, you move immediately to that address on the map and skip step 4.

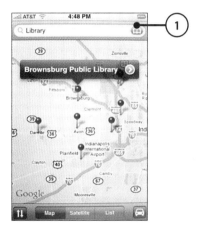

2. Press Contacts.

3. Browse the list of contacts.

4. Press the contact whose address you want to see on the map. The contact's information appears.

Lists Have a Good Memory

The Lists button remembers the last tab you used. If you most recently used the Recents list, the next time you press the Lists button, you move to the Recents list again.

5. Press the address you want to see on the map. You move back to the map, the address is marked with a push pin, and the contact's name is shown.

6. Use the information in the "Working with Maps" task to find out more information about the location and to change the map's view.

Finding a Location by Recent Searches

As you view maps, iPhone tracks the locations and searches you've used so that you can easily get back to a map you previously generated:

1. Press the Lists button.

Changed Your Mind?

If you don't want to use a recent item, press Done, and you move back to the map, which is not changed. To clear your recent list, press Clear. All recent items are removed from the list.

2. Press Recents. You see the list of searches and locations you've used recently.

3. Browse up or down the list.

4. To show the recent item on the map, press it. You move back to the map and the item (location, search, and so on) is shown.

5. Use the information in the "Working with Maps" task to find out more information about the location and to change the map's view.

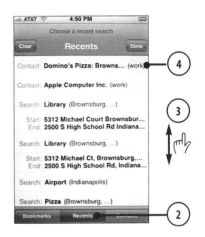

Finding a Location with Bookmarks

Bookmarks enable you to save locations and return to them easily. (See the called "Working with Maps" task to learn how to set bookmarks.)

1. Press the Lists button.

2. Press Bookmarks. The Bookmarks screen appears.

3. Browse up or down the list to see all the bookmarks available to you.

4. Press the bookmark you want to see on the map. You move back to the map, and the bookmarked location is shown. Use the information in the "Working with Maps" task to find out more information about the location and to change the map's view.

Deleting or Changing Bookmarks

You can remove bookmarks from the list, and you can change their information:

1. Move to the Bookmarks screen.

2. Press Edit. Unlock buttons appear for each bookmark along with the Edit and Order buttons.

3. To change the order of bookmarks, press a bookmarks order button and drag it up or down the list of bookmarks.

4. To delete a bookmark, press its Unlock button.

5. Press Delete. The bookmark is deleted from the list.

6. To change a bookmark's name, press it. The Edit Bookmark screen appears.

7. Use the keyboard to make changes to the bookmark's name.

8. Press Bookmarks. You return to the Bookmarks screen, and the changes you made to the bookmark's name are shown.

9. When you're done making changes, press Done. You exit the Edit mode and can work with bookmarks again, or press Done to return to the map.

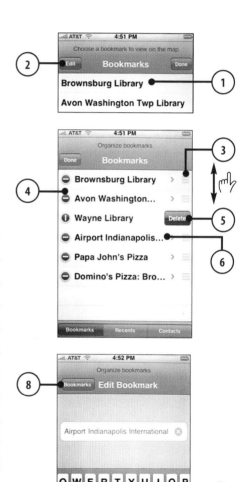

Working with Maps

After you find locations on a map, you can work with them for a variety of purposes:

1. Find locations in which you are interested using one of the techniques described earlier, such as a search, bookmark, and so on.

2. To zoom in on a location, double-press the map near the location or unpinch the map to move them apart.

3. To scroll the map, drag your finger up or down and left or right.

4. Double-press with two fingers to zoom out by a set amount or pinch your fingers together on the screen to control the amount of zoom.

5. Press a location's push pin. You see the name of the location.

6. Press the More Info arrow. The Info screen appears.

7. Use the information on the Info screen to call the location, view its website, or see it on the map.

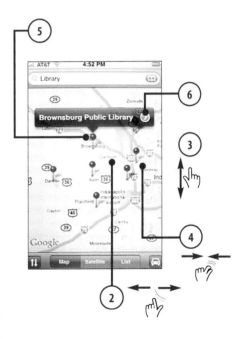

Show Them All

When your search has found more than one location on the map, press List to see a listing of all the locations shown. Press a location to jump to it on the map. This is helpful when you've done a more general search and you want to see all the results easily.

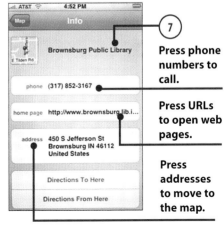

Press phone numbers to call.

Press URLs to open web pages.

Press addresses to move to the map.

8. Scroll down the screen.

9. To use the location in directions, press Directions To Here or Directions From Here. (See the "Getting Directions and Traffic Conditions" task for more information.)

10. To set a bookmark for the location, press Add to Bookmarks. The Add Bookmarks screen appears.

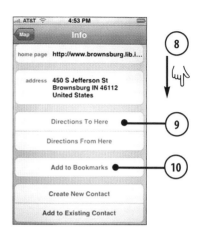

11. Use the keyboard to make changes to the bookmark's name.

12. Press Save. The location is added to your bookmarks and you return to the Info screen.

Hide a Location

To hide the location's name again, press it.

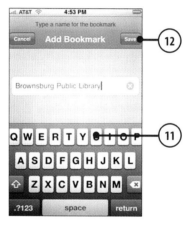

13. To create a new contact for the location, press Create New Contact. The New Contact screen appears.

14. Enter more information for the contact if desired. (For more information about entering contact information, see Chapter 2, "Managing Contacts.")

15. Press Save. The location is added to your contacts, and you return to the Info screen.

16. To add the location's information to an existing contact, press Add to Existing Contact. The All Contacts screen appears.

17. Browse the list to find the contact to which you want to add the location's information.

18. Press the contact to which you want to add the location's information. The location's information is added to the contact, and you see the changes on the contact's Info screen.

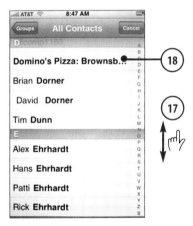

19. Press Map. You move back to the map and can work with other locations.

Buttons Change

The buttons you see on a location's Info screen depend on the status of that location. For example, if you've already added the location as a bookmark, the Add to Bookmarks button doesn't appear.

Getting Directions and Traffic Conditions

The Maps widget can generate directions between two locations and even show you the traffic conditions in the area.

1. Press the Directions button. The Start and End boxes appear.

2. Find the start location by searching for it or by using the Lists button to select it from a list. Finding a start or end location works just like finding any location. For example, you can use a bookmark, recent item, or contact information to set a location along with searching for a location.

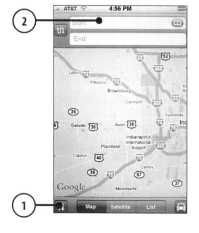

Can't Tell if You're Coming or Going?

You can start the direction process from a location's Info screen by pressing the Directions To Here or Directions From Here button to set that location as the starting point or endpoint.

3. Find the end location by search-
    ing for it or by using the Lists but-
    ton to select it from a list.

4. Press Route. A path from the start
    location to the end location is
    generated and appears on
    the map.

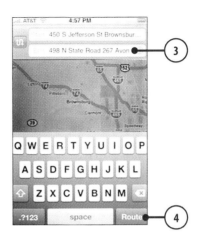

5. Zoom or scroll the map as need-
    ed to view the path.

6. To see a detailed list of each step
    in the directions, press List. Each
    segment along the way is shown.
    The highlighted segment indi-
    cates which is currently in focus
    on the map.

7. Scroll up and down the screen to
    see the complete list of steps.

8. To view the specific segment on
    the map, press it. The map appears
    and shows the segment you
    pressed. At the top of the map,
    you see the segment. The map
    shows the segment with any turns
    highlighted with a circle.

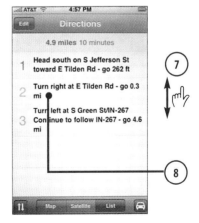

9. To move to the next segment, press the Forward button.

10. To move to a previous segment, press the Back button. When you move too far from the segment displayed, the map automatically scrolls and zooms to take you to the new segment.

No Directions Required

You can view the traffic conditions on the map at any time. (You don't have to generate directions first.)

11. To see traffic conditions, press the Traffic Conditions button. Roads are color coded according to available traffic information. Roads running 50 mph or more are coded in green. Yellow roads are running between 25 and 50 mph. Red roads are less than 25 mph. Gray roads have no information available. (Purple marks your route.)

12. To return to map mode, press the Directions button.

Going Back Again

To quickly reverse the current route, press Edit. Then press the Reverse button, which is located to the left of the Start and End fields.

It's Not All Good

Take the traffic condition information with a large grain of salt. The accuracy of this information depends on many variables, including the area you are viewing, how accurate the local reporting stations are, and so on.

Unfortunately, the Maps widget doesn't have built-in GPS capabilities, which is too bad because that would increase its value tremendously. Hopefully, it will be improved over time or a third-party widget for GPS for iPhone will become available soon.

Watching the Weather

The Weather widget is a handy way to get information about weather in specific locations quickly and easily.

>>>step-by-step

Choosing Weather Locations

Configure the Weather widget with the areas you are interested in:

1. Move to the Home screen and press Weather. The Weather widget appears.

Who needs The Weather Channel anymore?

2. Press the Info button. The Weather screen appears. On this list, you see all the locations that the widget currently shows.

3. To add a location, press the Add button. The Add Location screen appears.

4. Enter a city's name using the keyboard.

5. Press Search. Cities that match your search are shown.

6. To add a city to the widget, press it. You move back to the Weather screen, and the city you added is listed.

7. To delete city, press the Unlock button. The Delete button appears.

8. Press Delete.

9. Perform steps 3 through 8 until the list contains all the cities about which you want weather information.

10. To have temperatures displayed in degrees Fahrenheit press °F.

11. To have temperatures displayed in degree Celsius, press °C.

12. Press Done.

Viewing Weather Information

With iPhone, getting weather information is simple:

1. Move to the Home screen and press Weather. The Weather widget appears. You see weather for the last city you viewed.

2. To see weather for the next location, drag to the left or right.

3. To jump to a specific location, press its button. You have to know where the location is on the list; for example, if a city is third on the list, press the third button.

4. To move to a website about a location to view its weather, press the Yahoo! button. The web browser opens, and you move to the Yahoo! page for that city that provides more detailed weather information, event information, and so on.

Forecast   **Current conditions**

Last updated

Using the Calculator

The Calculator widget is very simple, but it can come in handy.

>>>step-by-step

1. Move to the Home screen and press Calculator. The Calculator widget appears.

Transform your iPhone into a $0.99 calculator.

2. Use its simple buttons to perform basic calculations.

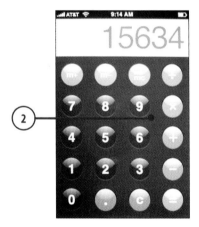

Working with Notes

Although it won't replace a word processor, the Notes widget is useful for capturing short notes while you are on the move. You can add notes and then read them later.

>>>step-by-step

Adding Notes

1. Move to the Home screen and press Notes. The Notes widget appears. You see existing notes, with the most recent at the top of the list.

Can't Spell Well?

As you type, iPhone's spell checker will identify misspelled words and make suggestions. To enter a suggested word, press the spacebar.

Microsoft Word doesn't need to be afraid.

2. Press the Add button. The New Note screen appears.

3. Type the note.

4. Press Done. The note is saved; you move to the note's screen, and you can work with it. (See the "Working with Notes" task for more information.)

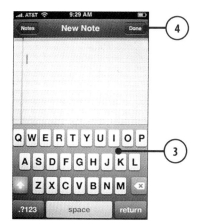

Working with Notes

1. Move to the Home screen and press Notes. The Notes widget appears. You see existing notes, with the most recent being at the top of the list.

2. Press the note you want to work with. The note's screen appears.

3. Read the note.

4. Press the Email button to send the contents of the note as an email.

5. Press the Trashcan button to delete the note.

6. To change the note, press its body. The keyboard appears.

7. Add text or make changes to existing text.

8. Press Done. The changes are saved, and you return to the note's screen.

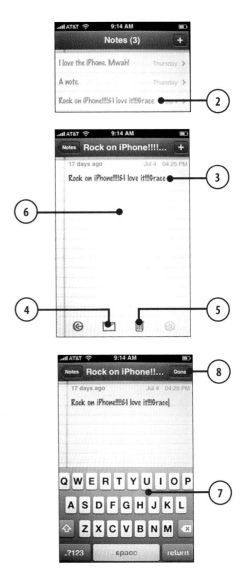

9. Press Back to move to a previous note.

10. Press Forward to move to a later note.

11. Press Notes to move back to the Notes screen.

Use Settings
to customize
your iPhone.

In this chapter, you'll explore the settings not related to specific iPhone functionality. The topics include the following:

→ Accessing iPhone settings

→ Using Airplane mode

→ Monitoring usage

→ Configuring general sound settings

→ Setting screen brightness

→ Setting wallpaper

→ Configuring general settings

Configuring iPhone's Settings

If you've read earlier chapters, such as the chapters on iPod or email functionality, you already have experienced configuring iPhone by using its Settings tool. Many of those settings relate directly to functionality discussed in other chapters. However, a number of iPhone settings are more general in nature, which is where this chapter comes into play.

Some examples of general settings you want to become familiar with include airplane mode (sets iPhone in "silent running" so that you can use iPod and other functions while you fly); sound settings (controls the noises iPhone makes); screen brightness (controls the brightness of the screen); and so on. While you might not use these functions everyday, they come in handy from time to time.

Accessing iPhone Settings

Scroll to see all settings.

To get to iPhone's settings, move to the Home screen and press the Settings button. The Settings screen appears; scroll to see and use all the settings available. The following sections describe various setting options and show you how to configure them.

Using Airplane Mode

Although there's a debate whether devices such as iPhone pose any real danger to the operation of aircraft, there's no reason to run any risk by using iPhone while you are on an airplane. (Besides, not following crew instructions on airplanes can lead you to less-than-desirable situations.) When you place iPhone in Airplane mode, its transmitter and receivers are disabled so that it poses no threat to the operation of aircraft. Of course, when you have permission to do so, you can use iPhone for iPod functions as well as all the other features that don't require connection to a network.

To put iPhone in Airplane mode, move to the Settings screen and press the OFF button next to Airplane Mode. The OFF button becomes ON; all connections to network servers, and iPhone goes into quiet mode in which it doesn't broadcast or receive any signals.

In Airplane mode, you can use iPhone for various functions, such as iPod, photos, and so on. To turn Airplane mode off, move to the Settings screen and press the Airplane Mode OFF button, which then becomes the ON button. iPhone resumes transmitting and receiving signals.

Indicates
iPhone is in
Airplane mode

Airplane
mode button

Monitoring Usage

The amount of call time and data usage that you accumulate on iPhone are recorded. You can view this information at any time.

>>>*step-by-step*

1. Move to the Settings screen and press Usage. The Usage screen appears.

2. Review the information in which you are interested, such as current period call time, which you can use to monitor the minutes you've used under your calling plan.

Charge
information

Call
information

EDGE data
information

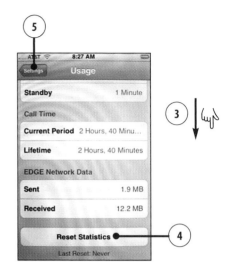

3. Scroll down the screen to reset monitoring.

4. Press Reset Statistics. The current statistics are reset, and logging begins anew (Lifetime Call Time information is not reset).

5. Press Settings to move back to the Settings screen.

Configuring General Sound Settings

You learned about most of iPhone's sound settings in Chapter 1, "Making, Receiving, and Managing Calls," and Chapter 3, "Listening to Audio and Watching Video." Two sound settings are more general to iPhone, and here's how to access and change them.

>>>*step-by-step*

1. Move to the Settings screen and press Sounds. The Sounds screen appears.

2. Scroll down the screen until you see the Lock Sounds and Keyboard Clicks settings.

3. Press Lock Sounds ON to disable the lock sound.

4. Press Keyboard Clicks ON to disable the sounds that iPhone's keyboard makes when you press its keys.

5. Press Settings. You move back to the Settings screen.

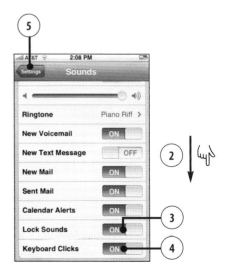

Setting Screen Brightness

Because you're continually looking at iPhone's screen, it should be the right brightness level for your eyes. However, the screen is also the largest single drain on battery power, so the less bright iPhone's screen, the longer iPhone's battery lasts. You have to find a good balance between viewing comfort and battery life. Fortunately, iPhone includes a brightness feature that adjusts for current lighting conditions automatically:

>>>*step-by-step*

1. Move to the Settings screen and press Brightness. The Brightness screen appears.

2. Press the ON button to disable the Auto-Brightness feature. You'll get more battery life with Auto-Brightness on, but the information is here in case you want to control the brightness manually.

3. Drag the slider to the right to raise the base brightness of the screen. This uses more power, but the screen is brighter.

4. Drag the slider to the left to lower the base brightness of the screen. This causes the screen to be dimmer but uses less power.

5. Press Settings. You move back to the Settings screen.

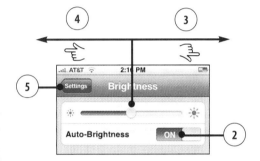

Setting Wallpaper

When iPhone is locked, you see its wallpaper. You can set the wallpaper for iPhone using either the default wallpaper collection or by choosing a photo you've moved onto iPhone.

>>>step-by-step

1. Move to the Settings screen and press Wallpaper. The Wallpaper screen appears. You see the sources of wallpaper available to you.

2. Press the source of wallpaper you want to view. The images in that source appear.

Using Your Photos as iPhone Wallpaper

To learn how to add photos to iPhone so that they are available as wallpaper, see Chapter 9, "Taking, Storing, and Viewing Photos."

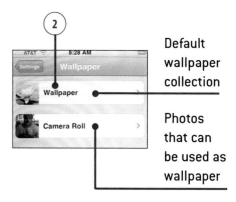

Default wallpaper collection

Photos that can be used as wallpaper

3. Press the wallpaper you want to use. You see a preview.

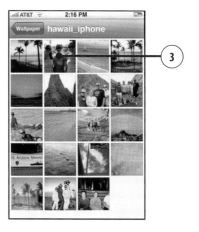

4. To set the wallpaper, press Set Wallpaper. You move back to the Settings screen. The next time iPhone is locked, you see the wallpaper you selected on the screen.

5. To choose a different wallpaper, press Cancel instead. You move back to the available wallpaper in the selected source.

Repeat steps 2 through 4 until you are happy with the wallpaper you selected.

Configuring General Settings

To configure iPhone's general settings, do the following:

>>>*step-by-step*

1. Move to the Settings screen and press General. The General screen appears.

2. Press About. You see the About screen.

Not All General Settings Revealed Here

This section does not describe all the general settings. Chapter 8, "Working with Date & Time and the Calendar," covers the Date & Time setting. Chapter 4, "Connecting to the Internet, Bluetooth Devices, and VPNs," discusses the Network and Bluetooth setting. Chapter 12, "Maintaining iPhone and Solving iPhone Problems," covers the Reset setting.

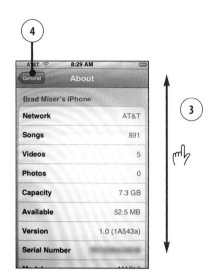

3. Scroll up and down the screen to view its information, such as the network, number of songs, videos, and photos, memory, software, serial number, and so on.

4. Press General to move back to the General screen.

5. Press Auto-Lock. The Auto-Lock screen appears.

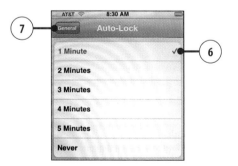

6. Press the amount of idle time you want to wait before iPhone automatically locks. You can choose from 1 to 5 minutes; choose Never if you want to manually lock iPhone. I recommend that you keep Auto-Lock set to a relatively small value to conserve your iPhone's battery.

7. Press General.

8. If you want a passcode to be required to unlock iPhone, press Passcode Lock. The Set Passcode screen appears.

9. Enter a four-digit passcode.

10. Re-enter the passcode. If the two passcodes match, you see the Passcode Lock screen.

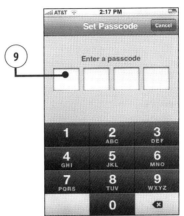

11. To require the passcode no matter how long iPhone has been locked, press Immediately; to set a 1-minute delay, press After 1 min. With a delay, if you accidentally lock iPhone and want to use it again, you can unlock it without a passcode as long as you do so within a minute or so.

12. To hide previews of messages you receive while iPhone is locked, press Show SMS Preview ON. The setting becomes OFF, and iPhone no longer previews messages for you when it is locked.

13. Press General. The General screen appears.

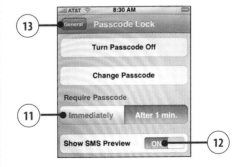

14. Press Keyboard. The Keyboard
screen appears.

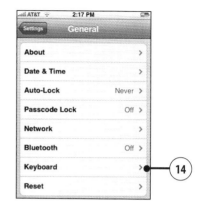

15. To prevent iPhone from automatically capitalizing as you type,
press Auto-Capitalization ON. Its
status becomes OFF, and iPhone
no longer changes the case of
letters as you type.

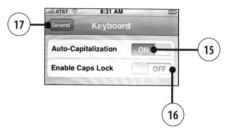

16. To enable the Caps Lock key, press
Enable Caps Lock OFF. The status
becomes ON, and when the keyboard appears, you can use the
Caps Lock key.

17. Press General. You return to the
General screen.

iPhone is easy to maintain and isn't likely to give you much trouble.

In this chapter, you'll learn how to keep iPhone in top shape and to know what to do should problems happen. Topics include the following:

→ Maintaining iPhone
→ Solving iPhone problems

Maintaining iPhone and Solving iPhone Problems

You see that this is a short chapter, and there is a good reason for that: iPhone works very well and you are unlikely to have problems with it, especially if you keep iTunes and iPhone's software current. When problems do occur, you can usually solve them with a few simple steps. If that fails, there's lots of help available for you on the Internet.

Maintaining iPhone

Some basic maintenance tasks keep iPhone in top working condition. Even better, you can do most of these tasks with just a couple of mouse clicks because you can configure iTunes to do most of the work for you.

Maintaining iTunes

As you've learned in this book, iTunes is a vital partner for iPhone. You should keep iTunes current to ensure that you have the latest bug fixes, new features, and so on. Fortunately, you can configure iTunes to maintain itself.

>>>*step-by-step*

Maintaining iTunes on Windows PCs

1. In iTunes, choose Edit, Preferences. The Preferences dialog appears.

2. Click the General tab.

3. Check the Check for updates automatically check box.

4. Click OK. The dialog closes. Periodically, iTunes checks for updates. When it finds an update, it prompts you to download and install it. Follow the onscreen instructions to do so.

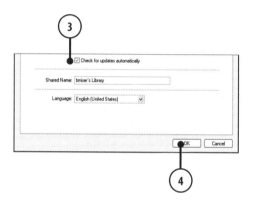

Check for Updates Now Windows

To check for updates at any time, choose Help, Check for Updates. iTunes checks for updates immediately. If you are using the current version, you see a message telling you so. If an update is available, iTunes prompts you to download and install it.

Maintaining iTunes on Macs

1. Open the System Preferences application.

2. Click Software Update.

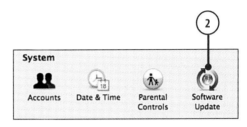

3. Check the Check for updates check box.

4. Choose the frequency that iTunes checks for updates on the pop-up menu.

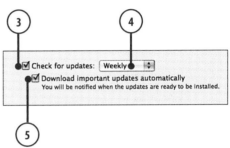

5. Check the Download important updates automatically check box.

6. Quit System Preferences. The Mac checks for updates for iTunes, along with all the other Apple software on your Mac, according to the timeframe you selected. When it identifies an update, it downloads the update automatically and prompts you to install it.

Check for Updates Now Mac

To check for updates at any time, open the Apple menu and choose Software Update. The Software Update application runs. If it finds an iTunes update, it prompts you to download and install it.

>>>*step-by-step*

Maintaining iPhone's Software

One of iTunes' iPhone functions is to maintain iPhone's software, which is one of the reasons you should keep iTunes current. Periodically, iTunes checks for new iPhone software. When iTunes finds updates, it installs them for you.

1. Connect iPhone to your computer.

2. Select your iPhone on the Source list.

3. Click the Summary tab. You see the current version of iPhone's software at the top of the screen.

4. Click Check for Update. If you're using the current version of iPhone's software, you see a dialog telling you so. If not, iTunes downloads the current version to your computer and prompts you to install it.

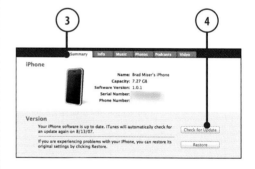

Maintaining iPhone's Battery

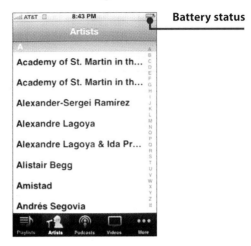

Battery status

Obviously, an iPhone with a dead battery isn't good for very much. As you use iPhone, you should keep an eye on its battery status. As long as the battery status is green, you're okay. As iPhone gets low on power, the battery on the status icon becomes empty and eventually turns red. Two separate warnings will alert you when the battery lowers to 20% and then again at 10%. If you keep going from there, iPhone runs out of power and shuts down. Of course, it gives you plenty of warning through onscreen messages before this happens.

This iPhone is charging.

The obvious way to prevent battery problems is to keep iPhone charged. The good news is that all you have to do is to connect iPhone to your computer and its battery charges. While this is occurring, and iPhone is locked, you see the large battery icon on iPhone's screen along with the charging icon in the upper-right corner of the screen. When charging is complete, the battery status icon reappears, the large battery icon disappears, and you see iPhone's wallpaper if it's locked or you see whatever screen you happen to be using if it isn't locked.

You can also connect iPhone to the external charger included in its box if your computer isn't handy.

Keeping iPhone Topped Off

It's a good idea to keep your iPhone's battery topped off; this type of battery actually does better if you keep it charged rather than letting it run down all the way before recharging. Periodically, say every month or two, you might want to let iPhone run completely out of power to maximize its life.

Cleaning iPhone's Screen

iPhone's onscreen controls are amazing. But because you use them by pressing and dragging your fingers on the screen, the screen gets smudges. You can clean the screen using the cloth included with iPhone. You should never spray any cleaners on iPhone's screen. However, you can apply a slight amount of glass cleaner to a very soft cloth and gently wipe iPhone's screen when it is extremely dirty.

Solving iPhone Problems

Even a device as good as iPhone can sometimes run into problems. Fortunately, the solutions to most problems you encounter are simple. If those simple solutions don't work, there's lots of detailed help available from Apple, and there's even more available from the community of iPhone users.

The problems that you can address with the simple steps described in this section vary and range from such issues as the iPhone hanging (won't respond to commands) to iPhone not being visible in iTunes (can't be synced). No matter which problem you experience, try the following steps to solve them.

Restarting iPhone

If iPhone starts acting up, restart it.

1. Press and hold the Sleep/Wake button until the red slider appears on the screen.

2. Drag the red slider to the right. iPhone powers down.

3. Press the Sleep/Wake button once. iPhone restarts, during which time the Apple logo appears on its screen. When the Home screen appears, try using iPhone again. If the problem is solved, you're done.

Restarting the Computer and iTunes

If iTunes can no longer see iPhone, restart the computer and open iTunes again.

1. Disconnect iPhone from the computer.

2. Restart the computer.

3. After the computer restarts, connect iPhone to it. iTunes should open and the iPhone should be selected on the Source list. If so, all should be well. If not, you need to try something else.

All USB Ports Are Not Created Equal

If your computer can't see iPhone when it's connected, try a different USB port. You should use a USB port on the computer itself rather than one on a keyboard or USB hub.

Resetting iPhone

If restarting iPhone or the computer doesn't help, try resetting iPhone using the following escalation of steps.

1. If iPhone doesn't turn on or freezes, press and hold the Home button down for at least 6 seconds. If an application was frozen, it quits and you return to the Home screen.

2. Restart iPhone using the earlier steps. If the problem goes away, you're done. If not, continue.

3. Press and hold down both the Home button and the Sleep/Wake button for at least 10 seconds. iPhone should turn off and then restart; you can release the buttons when you see the Apple logo on the screen. If the problem goes away, you're done. If not, continue.

4. If you can use iPhone's controls, proceed with the following steps. If not, you need to restore iPhone, which the next section explains.

5. On the Home screen, press Settings. The Settings screen appears.

6. Press General. The General screen appears.

7. Press Reset. The Reset screen appears.

8. Press Reset All Settings.

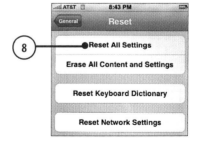

9. Press Reset All Settings. All settings on iPhone reset to their defaults and iPhone restarts. If the problem goes away, you're done—except for reconfiguring your settings, of course. If not, continue.

10. Repeat steps 5 through 8 to move back to the Reset screen.

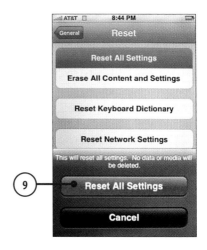

11. Press Erase All Content and Settings. When you do this, you lose all the content on iPhone. Make sure that you have that content elsewhere before you erase iPhone. If the content is in your iTunes Library, you're fine. But if you've added information that you have not synced to iTunes, such as contacts, directly onto iPhone, you lose that information when you erase iPhone.

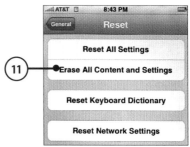

12. Press Erase iPhone. iPhone is erased, and it should return to like-new condition. You have to sync it again, reconfigure its settings, and so on. If the problem recurs, you must restore iPhone.

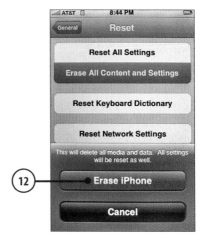

Restoring iPhone

The most severe action you can take on iPhone is to restore it. When this happens, iPhone is erased, so you lose all its contents and its current software is overwritten with the latest version. If none of the other steps corrected the problems, restoring iPhone should.

1. Connect iPhone to your computer.

2. Select iPhone on the Source list.

3. Click the Summary tab. You see the current version of iPhone's software at the top of the screen.

4. Click Restore. Remember that you lose everything on iPhone when you restore it, so make sure that you have all its data stored elsewhere before you do this.

5. Click Restore in the dialog. iTunes erases iPhone and reinstalls its software. This can take several minutes; iTunes displays progress dialogs along the way so that you know what's happening.

6. When the process is complete, click OK in the completion dialog. iPhone restarts and appears in iTunes just as when you first connected it to your computer. The Set Up Your iPhone screen appears.

7. Choose Restore from the radio button labeled backup of.

8. On the pop-up menu, choose your iPhone's previous name.

9. Click Continue. iTunes again resets iPhone and it restarts.

10. Click OK in the completion dialog. iPhone appears on the Source list in iTunes.

11. Using the steps in previous chapters in this book, reconfigure iPhone's settings, including synchronization options. You do this the same way you did when iPhone was new.

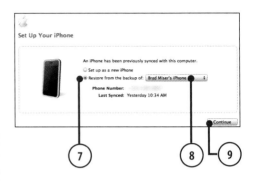

How Does It Remember My Phone Number?

You might wonder why and how you don't have to go through the activation process again. That's because iTunes backs up critical iPhone settings, such as activation information and some configuration settings, on your computer.

Reinstalling iTunes

If iTunes continues to be unable to see iPhone and iPhone appears to be working, reinstall iTunes on your computer. (This is much more likely on a Windows PC than on a Mac.) See the Prologue for instructions on downloading and installing iTunes on your computer.

No iTunes Content Worries

iTunes stores content, such as music and video, in a different location than the application itself. You can reinstall iTunes without disturbing your iTunes content. Of course, you should always have your iTunes content backed up, such as storing it on DVD, in case something happens to your computer.

Getting Help with iPhone Problems

If none of the previous steps solved the problem, you can get help in a number of ways:

- **Apple's website** Move to www.apple.com/support/. On this page, you can access all kinds of information about iPhone and other Apple products. You can browse for help, and you can search for answers to specific problems. Many of the resulting articles have detailed, step-by-step instructions to help you solve problems as well as links to more information.

- **AT&T's website** Move to www.wireless.att.com. You can get help with problems you're having with your connection to the AT&T network, and you can log in to your AT&T account to get information about it.

- **Web searches** One of the most useful ways to get help is to do a web search for the specific problem you're having. Just open your favorite search tool, such as Google, and search for the problem. You are very likely to find many resources to help you, including websites, forums, and such. If you encounter a problem, it's likely someone else has, too, and they've probably put the solution on the Web.

- **Me** You're welcome to send email to me for problems you're having with iPhone. My address is bradmacosx@mac.com. I'll do my best to help you as soon I can.

Index

X–Z

THIS BOOK IS SAFARI ENABLED

INCLUDES FREE 45-DAY ACCESS TO THE ONLINE EDITION

The Safari® Enabled icon on the cover of your favorite technology book means the book is available through Safari Bookshelf. When you buy this book, you get free access to the online edition for 45 days.

Safari Bookshelf is an electronic reference library that lets you easily search thousands of technical books, find code samples, download chapters, and access technical information whenever and wherever you need it.

TO GAIN 45-DAY SAFARI ENABLED ACCESS TO THIS BOOK:

- Go to **http://www.quepublishing.com/safarienabled**
- Complete the brief registration form
- Enter the coupon code found in the front of this book on the "Copyright" page

If you have difficulty registering on Safari Bookshelf or accessing the online edition, please e-mail customer-service@safaribooksonline.com.

Googlepedia: The Ultimate Google Resource, Second Edition

By Michael Miller

ISBN: 9780789736758 | 816 Pages

Googlepedia is not just for searching! Did you know that over the years Google has added a variety of features, services, tools, and businesses that make it a one-stop-shop for virtually any web user? This book takes you way beyond web searches by exposing you to Google's tools, services and features. *Googlepedia* provides comprehensive information that will benefit every Google user.

Now Available

iPodpedia: The Ultimate iPod and iTunes Resource

By Michael Miller

ISBN: 9780789736741 | 528 Pages

iPodpedia is the first book to show you everything that iPod and iTunes have to offer—from music to movies and beyond. Whether you want to get the most out of your iPod's music playback, create your own playlists, edit your music info and album art, convert your home movies and DVDs to iPod videos, listen to audiobooks and podcasts, or just unfreeze a frozen iPod, *iPodpedia* will show you how to do it.

Now Available

Photopedia: The Ultimate Digital Photography Resource

By Michael Miller

ISBN: 9780789737250 | 600 Pages

Photopedia is a comprehensive A to Z guide that includes instruction in both basic photographic techniques and advanced digital image manipulation. This is a full-color guide to all aspects of digital photography—from composing the shot, editing, printing or sharing the photograph. *Photopedia* is perfect for those new to digital photography and for traditional photographers who face a learning curve when switching to digital.

Available December 2007